• HAZELDEN MEDITATIONS •

She Recovers Every Day

Meditations for Women

DAWN NICKEL, PhD

Hazelden Publishing
Center City, Minnesota 55012
hazelden.org/bookstore

ISBN: 978-1-61649-993-8
Ebook ISBN: 978-1-61649-994-5

Library of Congress Cataloging-in-Publication Data

Names: Nickel, Dawn Dorothy, 1960– author.
Title: She recovers every day : meditations for women / by Dawn Nickel, PhD.
Description: Center City, Minnesota : Hazelden Publishing, 2023. | Includes index. | Summary: "A daily meditation book for women who are in recovery from addiction, cancer, workaholism, anxiety, abusive relationships, and more, written by the co-founder of the SHE RECOVERS® Foundation"—Provided by publisher.
Identifiers: LCCN 2022044842 (print) | LCCN 2022044843 (ebook) | ISBN 9781616499938 (paperback) | ISBN 9781616499945 (epub)
Subjects: LCSH: Recovering addicts—Psychology. | Healing. | Self-acceptance in women. | Women—Psychology. | Meditations.
Classification: LCC HV4999.W65 N53 2023 (print) | LCC HV4999.W65 (ebook) | DDC 362.29—dc23/eng/20221123
LC record available at https://lccn.loc.gov/2022044842
LC ebook record available at https://lccn.loc.gov/2022044843

Editor's notes

This publication is not intended as a substitute for the advice of health care professionals.

Hazelden Publishing offers a variety of information on addiction and related areas. Our publications do not necessarily represent Hazelden Betty Ford Foundation's programs, nor do they officially speak for any Twelve Step organization.

27 26 25 24 23 2 3 4 5

COVER DESIGN: TERRI KINNE
TYPESETTING: PERCOLATOR GRAPHIC DESIGN
DEVELOPMENTAL EDITORS: ANDREA LIEN, KAI BENSON, AND MARC OLSON
EDITORIAL PROJECT MANAGER: BETTY CHRISTIANSEN

"As a person in long-term recovery, my daily practice is pivotal to my overall well-being. This new collection of hope, healing, and inspirational passages will become part of my daily routine."

—Jennifer Storm, author of *Blackout Girl: Tracing My Scars from Addiction and Sexual Assault*

"I've often found myself in a tough situation and wondered, 'How would Dawn Nickel talk me through this?' This book is a treasure that allows us to spend time each day reflecting on words of wisdom from a trusted mentor who knows what it's like to live in recovery. "Mama Dawn" has all the best qualities of a cheerful neighbor, kind aunt, hilarious friend, and wise coach. She always knows just what to say to help others understand their personal capacity and potential."

—Jean McCarthy, host of *The Bubble Hour* podcast

"Dawn Nickel speaks to all—no matter what you're recovering from, the length of time you've had sustained recovery, and for those who have had a million stops and starts. She gives all of us permission to be so incredibly gentle and compassionate with our process of unfolding and recovery, which I believe is the first essential step—self-acceptance and self-compassion."

—Ester Nicholson, founder and CEO of Soul Recovery, trauma healer, She Recovers coach, trainer, and presenter

"*She Recovers Every Day* is a bookshelf staple to support your peace and your recovery. Providing a framework for your internal work, it offers tips and inspiration for your meditation practice and, most importantly, your relationship with yourself."

—Elena Brower, artist, poet, and best-selling author of *Practice You, Being You, Art of Attention,* and *Softening Time*

"Dawn has provided a tool for recovery from a place of love and generosity. This book is filled with reminders that we are not alone and that everything we need comes from within us. What a beautiful gift to those of us at all stages of recovery."

—Elaine Alec, author of *Calling My Spirit Back*

"Dawn gets it. These daily affirmations are full of practical guidance, real wisdom, humor, and grace. A tremendous resource for women in recovery."

—Laura McKowen, author of *We Are the Luckiest* and founder of The Luckiest Club

"As someone who is in active recovery from many things (aren't we all?) this book is a life-saving gem and one I refer to daily. There is no one like Dawn, and this book is a gift to the world."

—Jennifer Pastiloff, best-selling author of *On Being Human*

In loving memory of my mother,
Dorothy Mary Prosser (1932–2000),
who taught me that love passed down
through generations can be both
unconditional and imperfect.

Acknowledgments

I want to acknowledge with respect, gratitude, and humility the Lək̓ʷəŋən peoples on whose traditional and unceded territories I live, work, and recover. I am privileged and blessed to live in this breathtakingly beautiful place that I call home (now known as Victoria, British Columbia). I am inspired by my surroundings each and every day.

It's important that I acknowledge my privilege, as that privilege has dictated my access to health care and recovery resources. I identify as a white, cisgender, hetero, able-bodied, educated, feminist woman. I'm also Canadian, which means that I have access to universal health care and a (generally) supportive social safety net. Over the years I have been the recipient of welfare, free addiction treatment (though that's not much of a thing in Canada anymore), and excellent medical care to get me through a range of health care crises, including addiction, depressive and anxiety disorders, and cancer. Today I am in a position to afford a therapist or recovery coach when I need one, and truthfully, I need them on a pretty regular basis.

Having the support of other caring individuals is paramount to my recovery, and I am so grateful for all the incredible women who have shown up for me in my life. I thank my oldest friends Val and Mickey for not giving up on me during my period of active and destructive addiction, and I'm grateful to every woman since who has in some way modeled what healing and recovery is all about. The women in the Twelve Step program where I first found recovery along with the women in the She Recovers community have most influenced how I think about and practice recovery. Profound thanks go to the Sacred Pausers in particular and the entire team at the SHE RECOVERS® Foundation, including my daughter and co-founder, Taryn.

I have dreamed of being a writer for most of my life, but I learned how to write when I was a graduate student studying under Dr. Susan L. Smith. More recently, I've been able to hone my craft while working alongside my research and consulting partner Dr. Tracy Byrne. Thanks also to my Hazelden editors Andrea Lien and Kai Benson, not just for their editing superpowers, but for their constant encouragement.

This book, like my recovery, is a patchwork that respects and calls upon the work of other women who have written about recovery, both visionaries and academics. My influences have been many, including but not limited to women like Melody Beattie, whose groundbreaking work on codependency has been transformative for me and many millions of people; Jean Kirkpatrick and Charlotte Kasl, who were the first to suggest that women could look beyond the Twelve Steps to recover; Stephanie Covington's work on women, addiction, and trauma; and Janet Woititz and Tian Dayton, who led the way with their theories about adult children of alcoholics and dysfunctional families. My recovery, my thinking, and my writing have all benefited from the wisdom of the aforementioned.

Lastly but most crucially, I appreciate the opportunity to thank my family for their love, encouragement, and support for everything that I do related to recovery. My late father (George) was one of my greatest cheerleaders, and he was so proud of this book. I just wish he could have stayed long enough to hold it in his hands. I'm grateful and fortunate that my sister Debra also chose recovery and we get to be present with and for each other through the good and the bad. Thank you, Debra. My life partner, Allan, is also in recovery, which keeps life interesting, but truthfully, those who know us know that it's largely Allan who keeps me alive and functioning. He takes excellent care of me, our home, and our family, and he supports all of my recovery obsessions. Allan, I love you. I'm lucky to have children and grandchildren who remind me of what is most important in my life, and I learn from them daily. I chose a life in recovery because of my two daughters many, many moons ago. It was the right and only choice for me and for them. Ashley and Taryn, I hope that you are as proud of me as I am of you.

Foreword

One day I was mindlessly scrolling through Facebook, and I saw a pretty post with a quote that immediately caught my attention. It read:

> *And then one day she realized that the quality of her recovery depended upon her ability to practice radical self-care.*

I've been in recovery for a long time, and I've heard and read a lot, but the idea embodied in the quote blew my mind. I got excited. I printed it out. Stuck it on the wall in my office. Used it as group material at the treatment center where I work.

I eventually connected with the woman who wrote those words, and when I did, I knew Dawn was the real deal. I recognized that she really wanted to bring light and hope to a world of women who needed those exact things. Soon afterward, she invited me to speak about healing from trauma at the 2018 She Recovers Conference in Los Angeles. The energy in the hotel ballroom that weekend was electric, filled as it was with women from all over the world curious about how to deepen their recovery experience and embrace the invitation to radical self-care that had stopped my scrolling months before. It was a magical event, a true celebration of recovery and resilience. I met so many people who were searching for something in addition to or different from the usually prescribed (textbook) pathway to freedom. Recovery is a personal journey, and She Recovers gives us permission to explore what works best for us while learning from other women's stories what works for them. Although there are many paths to the top of a mountain, the destination is the same!

This little book is a culmination of some of Dawn's wisdom integrated with her incredible capacity for love and compassion. May it help many.

Mackenzie Phillips
Author, actor, treatment professional
Los Angeles

Introduction

For the first thirty years of my life, everything seemed to be on a spectrum of extremes. I went from being emotionally neglected to anxious, from abused to confused, from numbed out to strung out, from traumatized to depressed and at times suicidal. The fact that I survived my former self long enough to find recovery is slightly miraculous. Because I have unwrapped so many of the gifts that long-term recovery brings, I believe that I have a sacred obligation to pay something forward. It also seems like an urgently right time to do this. A growing women's mental health crisis means that the need to better identify and support all women in or seeking recovery has never been clearer.

Every single one of us has at least a thing or two that we need to address in order to live our healthiest, happiest lives. This truth is a cornerstone of what I believe about recovery; it's also the overarching principle guiding the women's recovery movement that I founded with my daughter Taryn. Since 2011, we have welcomed diverse people into the She Recovers community and met people where they are on their recovery journey by believing in and sharing the idea that we are all recovering from something. This daily meditation book is not about any one specific condition, addiction, or life challenge. Instead, it's designed to help you contemplate and even embrace the notion that you can take charge of your life and recover, no matter what you are recovering from.

I know that you can because I did.

If nobody has ever told you yet that you are worthy of living a happier and healthier life, let me be the first. Just hang in here with me, one day at a time. I'm going to share a little bit about what has worked for me. I also get to share a diverse patchwork of other women's voices, ideas, and experiences. I am committed to not telling other women what to think or to do when it comes to recovery—the foundation of building a self-directed recovery practice is always personal agency.

This book is a daily invitation to recover; it's also an invitation for you to define recovery for yourself. If this is your first invitation to recovery, welcome. If you are like I was when I first started to heal, you may be landing here quite tired, frustrated, confused, or scared. You may also be arriving here with hope and anticipation. Those feelings are valid too; all your feelings are valid, and in recovery you will learn your way around listening to and acknowledging them for what they are. I celebrate you showing up just exactly as you are.

If you've been doing this recovery thing for a long time but are feeling discouraged about how that's been going for you, or just are looking for new inspiration to tackle that next thing, welcome. I have found that bringing curiosity to new opportunities for growth is never a waste of time. You'll find that I'm exploring new frontiers of personal growth for myself too—and I have many conversation partners.

If you are a woman dearly attached to Twelve Step recovery in any of the hundreds of anonymous programs now in existence across the world, I want you to know that while I apply a critical lens to some aspects of anonymous programs, I am mostly interested in advancing ideas about how Twelve Step fellowships can do better for the women they serve. I come to this discussion as someone who loves, honors, and celebrates Twelve Step recovery despite having a recovery practice that is no longer steeped in it. Millions of people have been introduced to recovery primarily through an anonymous program, and that value cannot be disputed.

I will always be grateful that I am one of them.

Whatever brings you to this book of daily ponderings, my hope is that it can help you figure out what you want to recover from, how you will do it, and what success looks like uniquely for yourself. I wrote this book because I think it's important that we redefine recovery, that we reframe it to include more than just substance use. I identify as a woman successfully recovered from substance use, cancer, and domestic violence, and I'm still actively recovering from anxiety, grief, and workaholism. I am proud of my recovery, and I'm proud of you for contemplating it or living in it yourself.

I wrote a year's worth of meditations because I know that recovery is a practice, not an event. I believe that setting aside a few minutes every day to think about recovery can help us underscore our commitment to that practice. I hope that some of my reflections, and those of the women who've shared their wisdom with me, spark or cement your own thoughts about recovery and that you carry on this important conversation outside of this book. Your voice and your ideas matter and are needed in the women's recovery movement. We are always stronger together.

This book is my love letter to recovery. I hope that something in it touches your heart.

In love and sisterhood,
Dawn

A note:
When I refer to women, I mean cis and trans women, as well as nonbinary individuals who identify with women's communities, and I include women of all ages, races, ethnicities, abilities, and backgrounds.

JANUARY

• JANUARY 1 •

She Recovers

In September 2018, the incredible poet and meditation teacher Sarah Blondin shared an astonishingly lovely meditation that she wrote for our women's recovery community, She Recovers. It was aptly titled "She Recovers," and as you might imagine, everyone in the audience was moved to tears and gratitude as she shared it from our conference stage at the Beverly Hilton in Los Angeles. I practically weep every time I rewatch it on our YouTube channel. The meditation is about fifteen minutes long and is filled with a barrage of poignant thoughts and ideas, but one line above all the rest captures my heart and takes my breath away every time I hear Sarah read it. That line is "She recovers, because she learned how to love in the face of unlove." In the face of unlove. That's it. Despite feeling unloved when I was younger, or unloving to myself when I was in the depths of despair and addiction, I have recovered. I learned how to love. Myself. My past. I do not take my recovery for granted. I recognize it as both the privilege and the gift that it is. But also: I fought my ass off for it.

In the name of love and under the
umbrella of love, she recovers.

• JANUARY 2 •

Beginning Again

One of the most common social media posts I see in our women's online recovery group is the simple declaration "Day one . . . again." It's almost always followed up with a short narrative of defeat underscored with hopelessness. But I wonder what it would be like if we encouraged each other to celebrate making the decision to try again rather than confessing or apologizing for it. Maybe we could add an exclamation mark to our "back to square one" statements. Think about how different it feels to write or read "Day one . . . again!" Sharing pride in our tenacity rather than lamenting our new beginnings will surely breathe new resolve into our efforts.

If I've learned anything in recovery, it's that shame gets us nowhere and that success can only be ours if we don't give up. As author Elizabeth Gilbert reminds us, "You can measure your worth by your dedication to your path, not by your successes or failures."

I can decide to begin again, proudly.

• JANUARY 3 •

Stop the Behavior

Taking note of a behavior that I want (or need) to stop rarely (if ever) translates into the immediate ability to stop. Stopping requires time, thoughtfulness, and sustained effort. I start off by pondering or writing about the behavior and how it's hurting me or others. Then I think about how good I will feel when I stop doing it. I usually write or speak aloud my commitment to stopping, and I might tell another person for accountability. Finally, I come up with a replacement behavior. Throughout every step, I try to be mindful and always kind to myself. I accept that sometimes I may have to start stopping—all over again.

Kudos to you if you have been able to stop using a drug, food, a relationship, work, perfectionism, procrastination, shopping, or some other behavior to change the way you feel. If, on the other hand, you are currently struggling with something that you know needs to change, simply admit that truth to yourself for now. Congratulate yourself for being honest. Then think about it some more tomorrow.

We can stop the behavior one minute,
one hour, or one day at a time.

• JANUARY 4 •

Recovery Is Not Linear

Most of us who have achieved long-term recovery will tell you that our early recovery was made up of stops and restarts, regardless of what we are recovering from. Few people can stop an unhealthy behavior one day and never, ever pick it up again. Good for those who do, but they are as rare as unicorns. I'm thankful to have learned the value of stopping destructive behaviors and even more grateful to have been able to stay stopped for many years. I only got to this point by stopping the behaviors for one day here, an hour there, or, at times, one minute at a time. I'm okay with all the times that I couldn't stop something, because I know that recovery is a process, not an event. I hope you know that too. And I hope that if you stumble in your recovery, as I have done in mine, you remember to have compassion for yourself, not judgment.

I add up all the minutes, hours, and days
that I am moving in the right direction
and celebrate them all.

• JANUARY 5 •

Know Your Value

One of the symptoms of addiction is self-loathing, which translates effortlessly into low self-worth. What might this look like? We accept less monetary compensation than we should for our work or our services, often for much longer than we should. We lack the confidence to even ask for more money. Other times, we give our time away freely and unconsciously, forgetting that time is our most valuable asset and can never be replenished.

To illustrate the point even better, switch out words like *money* and *compensation* and *work* and *services* for other, less tangible things like *appreciation* and *respect* and *support* and *love*. This is to show that the greatest way we undervalue ourselves is not transactional and has little to do with jobs and money. It's about the inherent value that we place on ourselves. It's much easier for us to identify the value that others bring into our lives. We know their worth because they model their belief in themselves. We need to start believing in our own intrinsic value and treat ourselves accordingly. The people around us will fall into line once they see the price tag that we are putting on our own worth. And they will stop expecting discounts.

Slowly but surely, I am recovering my sense of self-worth and acting accordingly.

• JANUARY 6 •

Honesty

Until I got honest about my addiction to drugs and alcohol, my codependency, my workaholism, there was no hope that I would recover from any of these things. Honesty about the things that are harming us can come in fits and starts for some of us. It starts with self-honesty, the inner knowing, sometimes accompanied by a sinking feeling, that the jig is up, coupled with the inner knowing that something has got to give, go, or change. Maybe you remember when that moment was for you. The moment that you got honest with yourself.

The other moment, equally powerful, is when we speak our truth aloud to someone else. Sometimes we get honest with a partner, another family member, a friend, a physician, or a therapist. Other times we share in a meeting full of strangers. Who did you get honest with, for the first time? It's also possible that you haven't had either of these moments of honesty yet. That's okay. Each in our own time.

Getting honest with ourselves and then
getting honest with others are big steps.

• JANUARY 7 •

Life Is Not a Test

There was a time in my life when every question or opportunity in front of me felt like a test that I was unlikely to earn a good grade for. That aligned with my belief that life was out to get me and that I would bomb where others would soar. Looking back, I realize what a paranoid and punishing perspective that was. I'm grateful that I no longer feel that way. It's true that we might freeze when presented with multiple choices about something that matters to us, but we can lean into that pause and feel our way to the right response. On an ongoing basis, we are called upon to sort out what is true and what is false, which is tricky in today's world, but we can research and discern what is truest for ourselves. Our character can be tested by people or events, but we can always respond kindly and authentically (okay, maybe not always). Life isn't a pass-or-fail endeavor. We always get marks for effort.

Life is just life. If I'm breathing,
I'm making the grade.

• JANUARY 8 •

On Abstinence, Broadly Speaking

I've learned that how other people recover is none of my business and deserves none of my judgment. For the first decade or so of my recovery from substance use, I was adamant that recovery could only be called recovery if a person was completely abstinent from all substances. I mean, I really, really insisted that was the case. Then, as now, I fully support abstinence-based recovery. I choose it for myself. I respect that committed members of Twelve Step programs choose it for themselves too. But I no longer believe that everyone must be abstinent to recover.

Recovery from a substance use disorder is about so much more than the substances we ingest, and abstinence as the basis of a universal definition of recovery fails to account or allow for individual contexts and experiences. A rigid commitment to the ideal that only abstinence equals recovery leaves out too many people—people who may not be abstinent but are still working hard at doing better and becoming healthier. Not respecting other people's pathways is problematic at best, and potentially fatal at worst.

Substance use recovery happens along a continuum, and I can choose where I fit along it.

• JANUARY 9 •

On Abstinence for Me

In early recovery, I made a commitment to being completely substance-free. I wasn't invited to consider any other pathway (that's a different story). When I found recovery, I was ready to follow an abstinent pathway because I needed to do something different, having already (unsuccessfully) tried to moderate my substance use for ten years at that point.

So I set out to quit everything completely, but I couldn't do it. I was able to give up cocaine, alcohol, and benzodiazepines (and never pick them up again), but for the first several years of my recovery, I smoked marijuana. That was my harm reduction period, and I'm grateful for that two-year bridge to abstinence because it took me those years to become ready to live in full-blown reality, to feel my feelings, to deal with my wounds and my traumas. That was my version of harm reduction. Yours could be different; I don't know. But I know this: harm reduction can save lives. It saved mine.

When it comes to recovery,
I'll do me and you do you.

• JANUARY 10 •

Recovering from All the Things

Today, I consider myself recovered from a substance use disorder, cancer, and domestic violence. The laundry list of things that I am *still recovering from* is mostly manageable, most of the time. I identify as being in active recovery from trauma, workaholism, anxiety, and perfectionism—with a lingering touch of codependency to keep life interesting. I've been doing recovery for a very long time, and thankfully, by this point in my life I have learned to listen to my intuition and know when I need to peel back another layer in my recovery. To keep growing, I generally do a lot of research and ask others for help and direction. I like to have a lot of different options when I am embarking on a new level of growth. My recovery is always going to be a patchwork built upon intuition first, with a bit of concerted personal effort, elements of other women's recovery journeys, and a dash of professional guidance thrown in. It's a practice, so I just keep practicing.

We are all recovering from something.

• JANUARY 11 •

Acknowledge Resilience

I often forget how resilient I am. I see someone else experiencing a personal hardship or a tragedy, and I think, *How on earth are they doing it? How are they able to get out of bed every morning? How are they* smiling? *I would never survive.* I forget that I have survived some very hard things myself. Addiction. Domestic violence. Cancer. Losing my mother and others whom I loved.

Resilience doesn't mean that we don't experience heartache and hardship; it means that bad things happened to us and we are still here. When we are in the eye of our storm, we don't realize we are growing stronger, but we are. Look around you. The women who have experienced severe challenges are often the most courageous, most inspiring women you will ever know. Now, reflect on your own past for a moment. It isn't very comfortable to revisit the darker times in our lives, but think for just a moment how miraculous it is that you are here now. Focusing on your recovery. Doing the best that you can, despite all that you have been through.

I am still here. And you are too.

Hold On; Pain Ends

I'm forever grateful for the small seed of hope that another recovering woman planted in me very early in my recovery. I was brand-new and crying my eyes out in a Twelve Step meeting, unable to comprehend what others were sharing until I heard a woman explain that the four letters in the word *hope* stood for "hold on; pain ends." By that time in my life, I'd been telling myself to just hold the hell on for years. My ears perked up. I hadn't thought about hitching my wagon to the idea of hope prior to that moment, but something about the sincerity in her voice convinced me to just give hope a try. That seed of hope kept me coming back for more, and the hope multiplied. The pain lifted enough that I started to hope that one day I might even be okay, and eventually I was.

If you are feeling hopeless and desperate about something in your life today, please hold on. Pain ends. A wise woman once told me so.

There's a reason that hope is called
the gateway drug to recovery.

• JANUARY 13 •

Reaching Out

It took me years to master it, but now I'm good at reaching out for support when I need it. Being a member of a lot of recovery groups on social media means that I can share what's going on for me any time of day or night and know that someone, somewhere will acknowledge and respond to me. Back in the day (I sound so old), we used to have to pick up an actual phone and dial a number. I'm not talking cell phones here; I mean actual house phones with heavy handsets and even rotary dialing. Technology makes reaching out easier these days, but it's still one of the hardest things that we do in recovery.

The best advice that I've ever heard about this is to practice reaching out when things are going well. Practice just saying "hey" to people you are connecting with in your recovery circles. Doing so will help pave the way for you to reach out when you are in distress.

I feel honored when women reach out to me for support. I will return the favor.

• JANUARY 14 •

Inching toward Our Dreams

Even in recovery, it can be easier to stay in dreaming mode than it is to do the work to make a dream come true. Then one day, we just know it's time to go for it. At that point, we learn or remember that the dream needs a plan, and the plan needs to be translated into lists, each one of which needs to be broken down into dozens or hundreds of baby steps. When we look at the big picture, we get overwhelmed. There's only one way forward. We take one small, easy baby step. And the next day, we take the next baby step.

When babies start walking, they wobble and sometimes fall. We can wobble and fall too, but we keep getting up, and we keep moving forward. Sometimes we ask somebody to hold our hand to steady us. As we build up our confidence, we take bigger steps and inch ever closer to making our dream come true.

My dreams will be accomplished one baby step at a time. I'll celebrate each baby step I take in the direction of my dreams.

To-Do (and Not-to-Do) Lists

I couldn't organize much in my life before I got into recovery, but shortly after I stopped using drugs, I replaced some of my substance-related rituals with a list-writing ritual. I've since become a spectacular list maker. When I need to complete or accomplish a project, I grab one of my pretty pens and my lovely lined notepad and settle down to get organized. There's just something about writing down things "to do" that speaks to me. Writing a list brings me great satisfaction, almost as much as completing everything on it. But there's another side of list writing for me, and that is that making lists can also feed my tendency to overwork or overdo in my life. At those times, I need to practice another ritual of mine—writing a "not-to-do" list. As with all things recovery, finding balance also means not overdoing things that I love to do.

Writing lists feeds my need for order and helps me stay organized, but it can also feed my tendency to want to do too much.

• JANUARY 16 •

Morning Rituals

My name literally means "break of day," so it makes sense that early morning holds special meaning for me. Over the past several years, I have become very intentional about the first hour or so of every day, in large part inspired by what other women in recovery have shared about the benefits of their own morning rituals. I've listened carefully, tried on different things, and designed my own nurturing morning practice.

I get up at 5:30 a.m. to enjoy quiet, solo time. I don't like being rigid, so the order in which I do things varies, but the things I do are very consistent. There is always a decaf latte and ten to twenty minutes of sitting in silence, which may or may not take the form of meditation. I write or journal, read from a daily meditation book, and pull a tarot card. I top everything off with a scalding hot shower. Toward the end of the shower, I pour a few drops of essential oil into the palms of my hands, rub them together, breathe in the vibrant scent, and say a prayer of thanksgiving.

Morning rituals, big or small,
get my day started on the right foot.

Triggers Gonna Trig

I don't remember anybody in my treatment center talking to us about triggers when I first got into recovery. I don't know if there was a lot of knowledge about triggers at that time. Maybe they just talked to us about our habits, or things they knew would worry or scare or upset us. I recall being told to avoid people, places, and things that could lead us back to using substances. But I don't remember the word *trigger* being used.

Now we know all about them. The trick is to figure out how you're going to respond to triggers when they happen, because inevitably they will. If you're new in recovery, you can identify a list of things that you know are going to send you out of your mind. And then you can come up with a plan for how you're going to react when those triggers arise. Being prepared is absolutely your best tool to deal with triggers. At the end of the day, there's nothing you can do to stop them. But you don't have to let them take you down.

Pay attention to what sends you out of
your mind; those are your triggers.

Life Is Full

As a recovering workaholic, I have had to closely examine my attachment to busyness. In the not-too-distant past, I was addicted to being busy—and to complaining about being busy. Busy was my badge of honor, and it made me feel important when very little else did. Explaining how busy I was to others kept them at a distance, which in turn enabled me to work more.

Today, I try not to use the word *busy*, but it still slips out of my mouth now and then. What I try to say instead is simply that life is full. Because it truly is. My life is made up of work, play, passion projects, time with people I care about in and out of recovery, and as much time alone as I can carve out. It can be a lot, but viewing and talking about my life as full (rather than busy) brings me into a place of gratitude as soon as the words are out of my mouth.

I am grateful for my full but spacious life.

• JANUARY 19 •

Tea as Tradition

Nothing makes me quite as happy as a hot, sweet cup of tea. My Irish grandmother and my mother taught me that stopping for a cup of tea was a sacred, necessary pause for the women in our family. Having a small cup of milky tea was a treasured treat when I was a small girl; being invited to sit at the table and drink a full cup at age twelve was a true rite of passage. When I was fifteen, my new best friend Val taught me that tea drinking was even cool for teenagers in social settings. Nobody else in our crowd bought into that radical notion, but we bonded over tea then and still do.

Tea is one of my self-care rituals, a daily constant that sustains me and always brings me joy. I'm grateful to the women in my life who taught me that it would.

A cup of tea can be so much more than
just a beverage, if you let it.

Finding Hope

Since devoting myself to recovery, I've never been without hope. I've experienced some really dark times in recovery, and there have been times when hope was all that I had. There's an Italian proverb that says "Hope is the last thing ever lost." How beautiful. How inspiring. I now understand that sharing hope is the most important thing I can do. Hope can be planted like a seed. I confess I was once a dope dealer; now I'm a hope dealer. I can share my experience and my knowledge to inspire hope in others. I can show them how to share their hope. And hope will spread. Hope will grow.

Hope is really about believing that things just might be okay. We can hope for healed relationships. We can hope for fresh starts. We can hope to make it through the next hour, next day, next week, next month, and next year in our recovery. We can hope to feel joy again. Hope means glimmers of light in the darkness, in the darkest of despair.

We all have hope. Somewhere. We might have to dig deep, but it's there.

• JANUARY 21 •

Yes . . . And

The "yes . . . and" principle is something that I pull out frequently to help balance my heart and my thinking. Yes, I am a gentle, patient, and warm woman, and I'm also a badass warrior who can rage against the patriarchy. Yes, you have messed up some things royally due to your addiction, and you are also a strong sounding board and support for other people who are messing up. Yes, we need to be in community and connection in order to grow and heal, and we also need solitude and introspection to move beyond the things that can still cause us grief.

I try to use "yes . . . and" to replace my instinct to say "yes . . . *but*." "Yes . . . but" shuts people and ideas down. Example: "Yes, you want to try to practice moderation with your drinking, but you won't be able to for long, and you will find yourself back in self-loathing again." Contrast that with "Yes, you want to practice moderation, and you know that you need to find strong support and a different approach to be successful in the long term." In the latter, "and" joins ideas together positively. Can you practice "yes . . . and" today?

Two things can be true at once, even if they are seemingly opposite.

A Deeper Wisdom

Many years ago, when I was new to recovery and enrolled in a women's studies program that made me question everything about everything, I did some research into alternatives to the Twelve Step program that was, despite its outdated and male-dominated language, still working for me. I found a few different frameworks, including a rewriting of the Twelve Steps by Patricia Lynn Reilly packaged as *A Deeper Wisdom: The 12 Steps from a Woman's Perspective*. Patricia, who had found her own recovery with regard to food, beautifully revises each of the twelve traditional Steps, but I've always been partial to her reinterpretation of Step Two. In AA, the Second Step reads, "Came to believe that a Power greater than ourselves could restore us to sanity." Fair and true enough, in my case. But Patricia's presentation is more inclusive and works better for those who might be hesitant about the higher power concept. Her version of Step Two reads "I have come to believe in the deep wisdom of my own inner life. I stop flailing and am restored to the sanity of a loving and respectful relationship with myself." How powerful is that?

I trust my own wisdom to bring me back into alignment with myself.

• JANUARY 23 •

Being in Remission

Why is no consideration ever given to the idea that the end point of the process of recovery from addiction could be that one is *recovered*? Not just "in recovery" but "recovered." There's a difference. Even those of us who achieve that current "gold standard" of substance use recovery—abstinence—are never considered to have achieved *remission*. How do we feel about that?

I celebrated being in clinical remission from cancer after I had been cancer-free for five years. It was a very big deal for me, as it is for many people who achieve five years free from cancer or another medical condition. Yet, despite decades having passed since I took a substance to change how I feel, I don't get to claim to be *recovered*. Even though substance use and mental health disorders are often considered diseases, it is not acceptable for me to say "I am in remission from a substance use disorder." How much further along might we be in eradicating shame and stigma if people could, after five years, declare that they are recovered from their disorder? Just thinking out loud, here.

How we speak about ourselves
and our recovery matters.

At the End of the Day

One of the recovery practices that I was introduced to early in my recovery was the practice of reflecting on my day before I go to sleep at night. I don't always remember to do it, but when I do, it really is an empowering and informative practice. In the evening, look back over your day before you close your eyes and recognize the moments where you absolutely got something right, and reflect upon areas where you know you want to do better tomorrow. Do a quick gratitude list in your head. Don't beat yourself up for where you fell short in your day; that's not the point of it. Awareness precedes growth. So just be aware.

One of my favorite quotes speaks directly to this concept and practice. Ralph Waldo Emerson wrote, "Finish each day and be done with it. You have done what you could; some blunders and absurdities have crept in; forget them as soon as you can. Tomorrow is a new day; you shall begin it serenely and with too high a spirit to be encumbered with your old nonsense." Old nonsense indeed. Let it go, and tomorrow build on your strengths.

In our daily inventory, we count our blessings and identify opportunities for growth.

• JANUARY 25 •

Rediscovering Recovery

I have fallen in love with recovery a few times in my life. The first was when I found and joined a Twelve Step program in my late twenties. I'd had no idea that I could live a life without substances and chaos, and I loved my new friends and life. I slowly drifted away from that program after about six years. I stayed abstinent but stopped doing the work of recovery, of self-discovery. Later, when my baby sister hit a hard bottom in addiction, I returned to that program to introduce it to her, hoping it would save her life too. It did, and I found myself enamored with recovery again. I recommitted and experienced another personal growth spurt, which came in handy when I nearly died from cancer. After cancer, I moved away from recovery again, this time toward workaholism. And after six years of overworking, I hit an intensely hard bottom and chose recovery again. My healing has looked vastly different over the past decade or so than it did in its first few iterations, but I love it as much as ever.

We can breathe new life into our recovery, and we should.

H.A.L.T.

If you have spent much time around people in recovery, then you will know that slogans and acronyms are a thing. Some are mildly annoying, but some are quite powerful. For example, the acronym H.A.L.T. is one of the most useful recovery tools I picked up in early recovery, and I still use it frequently. H.A.L.T. works like a built-in self-care warning system. The idea behind it is that when you are feeling vulnerable in your recovery or even just out of sorts in general, you can stop and ask yourself if you are hungry, angry, lonely, or tired. If the answer to any of those questions is yes, then that thing needs to be addressed. Taking a catnap, if possible, will do wonders if you are tired, and a snack or meal will fix your hunger. The best antidote for loneliness is a visit or call with a close friend, and anger might require that you deal with whatever is making you mad, or at least take a brisk walk to displace the negative energy. H.A.L.T. is a brilliant tool, in my view. Were you familiar with it before now?

Stopping to check in with ourselves
is always a good practice.

• JANUARY 27 •

Letting Go of Regret

I try hard not to have regrets in my life, small or large. Unfortunately, being human and all, I still do things that I wish I hadn't, or don't do things that I wish I had. I probably always will. But if the regrets mount up, I hope that I do what my mom did as she was nearing the end of her life. She shared with me a few of her most painful regrets. There was absolutely nothing she could do to change the things that she did or didn't do, but I could sense her spirit getting lighter as she shared them. I also got to share back that I was okay with the things she talked about that affected me personally. I was able to ask her to let them go. I like to think she did. I hope she did.

I can't change the past, but I can let go
of my attachment to regrets about it.

• JANUARY 28 •

A Few Things I Learned in Therapy

I've been very privileged to be able to access a lot of therapy over the decades of my recovery, including free therapy. I hope that if you need therapy, you can access it. I'm one of those odd specimens who really loves therapy, even though it's often hard. Scratch that: it's *always* hard. But so far, it's always been worth it. The things that I have learned about myself in therapy have changed my life.

Here's my short list of things learned: Hearts broken in childhood take a lot of time to heal. Missing someone is not the same as grieving someone (now, that one blew me out of the water). Anger is almost always inner pain turned outward. I like to mother the people I love (could be responsible for my nickname, Mama Dawn). I don't like goodbyes (builds on an earlier insight from therapy that I don't like transitions). I can and prefer to love unconditionally, but I couldn't always do that. Getting to know these things about myself has been life changing. I'm excited to keep going, to keep learning more about who I am and what I want and how I want to show up in this lifetime.

It's okay to seek therapy before it seeks you.

Past as Prologue

As much as I don't love that this is true, there is a predictable pattern that unfolds before I find myself sunk back into my workaholism. It usually goes something like this: I forget how much I love my life when it is spacious and I have the time to read the novels, play with the grandkids, and go for drives with the husband. I forget to think carefully before I say yes to some other contract, project, or exciting shiny thing that is happening in our She Recovers community. I realize that I am going to have to juggle more than I want to juggle. Then I get anxious. I start juggling more than I want to juggle. I feel inadequate, I fear that I will let somebody down somewhere along the way, and I pick up speed, moving into hyper-competent mode. I get up earlier and stay up later to work. I begin to burn out. I remember I am a workaholic, and I stop. I re-evaluate. I disappoint someone, probably. But I regain my footing and my life, and I go on. More slowly. I feel the grace of having survived myself again.

I can disrupt the pattern earlier, but I've not figured out how to stop it completely yet.

Recovering from Infant Loss

My dear friend Lisa has shared so much with me about the deepest sorrow that a parent can experience: the loss of a child. When Lisa and her lovely husband welcomed their son, Rowan, they were grateful to share a few breaths earthside with him. Years later, Lisa struggles to describe losing Rowan. As she reflects, "What word is there, really, to describe the experience of deeply loving someone you had never met but know better than anyone who had come before?"

Lisa generously shares her experience of profound loss to help other women know that if they are recovering from infant loss—or the loss of a child at any age—their loss is valid; their pain is real. As Lisa reminds us, grief isn't something you get over. It is something you move through. Lisa isn't looking for closure over losing Rowan; she doesn't believe she will ever have it. She knows that every year, the changing of the seasons, the anniversary of his death, and the date he was due to come into the world will be marked in her heart. She will hold the sacred memories of feeling his skin against hers. Forever.

Grief lives on as long as love does.
We move through it gently.

• JANUARY 31 •

Tiny Giants

Carley, one of our She Recovers community members, regularly refers to her three little children as her "tiny giants" when she shares at our online meetings. Curiosity got the better of me recently, and I asked her why she called them that. Carley disclosed that back when she was actively self-medicating, she would refer to them as her little monsters, because so much of what they did felt like a monstrous assault on her nervous system. In recovery, she began to feel all her feelings, acknowledge the traumas she had been hiding from, and, over time, nurture her body and clear out her mind. New realizations soon followed, including one that her sweet little babies were not in fact monsters out to get her; they were simply giant souls in tiny bodies, learning about their world and themselves. Just like Carley—and all of us—they are truly doing the best they can. Today, Carley expresses deep gratitude for all the gifts and the lessons that she receives from being a mother to her tiny giants.

Perceptions and outlooks change in recovery,
and benefits soon follow.

FEBRUARY

Doing Our Own Work

If women from all backgrounds are to heal, if women of color are to be empowered to build the recovery practices that are right for them, then *all* women need to participate in the project of healing racism within recovery communities. We do the work so that our recovery spaces are safe for women who have been impacted by systemic racism, abuse, and related traumas. Why am I talking about racism on this day and in this book? you ask. Because racism is trauma, and trauma has everything to do with recovery. It's impossible for real recovery to take root if we're perpetuating trauma in others' lives.

If you are a white woman in recovery, will you join in as the rest of us white women educate ourselves, then start talking about and dismantling the role of white privilege and other systems of privilege in our lives? The trick to doing the work is to start with the open-ended question "How am I racist?" Because we all are, in some way. Like other areas of recovery, admitting we have a problem is the first step.

All women deserve recovery.

Respect All Pathways

I am someone who loves, honors, and celebrates Twelve Step recovery despite having a recovery practice that is no longer steeped in it. When people who are more committed to working an anonymous program feel compelled to point out how poorly I am working (or not working) my program, I remind them that the only requirement for membership in my program is the desire to stop acting on my addiction. Come to think of it, that's true for all Twelve Step programs. When people judge my recovery, they generally judge me for not doing my recovery their way. I've said it elsewhere and I'll say it again: how I recover is nobody's business except my own. Early in my recovery, I was prone to easily feeling shame and guilt if I didn't do recovery the way that others expected me to. Shame and guilt were comfortable feelings for me when I started out. As I grew in my recovery and my approach to wellness expanded, I stopped caring what other people thought about how I was healing. I feel only pride in how I do recovery today. And so should you. Always.

There's no room for shame
in the recovery game.

• FEBRUARY 3 •

Bend before You Break

Bending before you break is about compromise. It's about giving up something to gain something else. There's a negative view toward compromise that implies compromising is somehow being weak. But it's not. When I compromise, I'm thinking about someone else's needs *as well as* my own, not *versus* my own. Compromise is about giving and taking. In relationships, it's about not being completely rigid, stubborn, intransigent, or inflexible. It's about delving into the art of compromise, flexibility, and negotiation. This concept isn't about bending your values or principles. There are times when you should stand strong, and there are things that you should never compromise on or find middle ground about. You will know what those are when they present, if you trust your intuition.

Trees bend. We can take guidance from artist Joanne Raptis: "Be like a tree. Stay grounded, connect with your roots, turn over a new leaf, bend before you break. Enjoy your unique natural beauty and keep growing."

In recovery, compromise is life. May we all be flexible when we can be and strong when we need to be.

• FEBRUARY 4 •

From Manifesto to Movement

My daughter Taryn and I refer to the She Recovers movement as our "accidental movement." We never set out to start it, but we are grateful that some of what we had to say so many years ago sparked something for so many women in or seeking recovery. We trace the movement's beginnings back to our Facebook page and a brief manifesto that I drafted to capture what I thought a women's recovery practice could look like. In that document, I suggested that "She Recovers" when

- She is encouraged to choose her own recovery path.
- She creates a vision for how she wants her life to be.
- She takes small and steady steps toward her vision.
- She makes peace with her past.
- She finally understands that self-care is the secret to her recovery.

Taryn and I shared the manifesto widely on our social media channels between 2012 and 2017, and those five ideas resonated with a lot of women. They informed our current set of ten Intentions & Guiding Principles, which now underpins everything. We might have started the conversation, but the movement itself is a co-creation of thousands of women across the world. We are so glad you are part of it.

Everybody's ideas about recovery matter. Together, we can paint a canvas of the possibilities.

• FEBRUARY 5 •

Sugar and Spice (Heavy on the Spice)

I write this for a beloved little girl who holds my heart in her hands, and I say it to your inner child too, in case she needs to be reminded. Don't ever lose your unique spirit. You know exactly what you want, and you aren't afraid to tell us. You barter and negotiate and fight mightily to get your way. You are persistent in all of your positions, and conceding isn't something that you always manage gracefully. You are loyal and protective, and your love is loud, even when you are screaming that you hate us. You have big feelings; joy oozes out of you in one moment, and big, cascading tears can flow down your cheeks in the next. You know that your tears break our hearts, and you don't hesitate to use that to your advantage. Your smile, though. It lights up our lives. Let your free spirit guide you; we will always be at your side to care for and celebrate you every step of the way forward.

Little one, watching you rise into who
you are meant to be is truly an honor.
Keep growing and glowing.

• FEBRUARY 6 •

The Art of Saying No

My life has improved immensely since I learned how to say no. I say it often. I'm still someone who comes through for people I care about when I'm asked to do something, but I no longer reply to requests with an automatic "Yes, of course I will." I've learned to stop and think through the pros and cons of saying yes, especially related to requests for my time. Being in recovery means that I lead a very full life, and I can't do everything that everyone else needs or expects me to do. I've had to learn how to prioritize my time and resources in my own best interests and in the interests of those closest to me.

When was the last time you said yes to something that should have been a no? How did that turn out for you? Did it mean less time or attention to the things that were important to you? Did you become resentful of the situation or the person you said yes to? Can you practice the art of saying no? Try it out. Today.

I am a truer version of myself
when I practice saying no.

• FEBRUARY 7 •

Toxic Ultra-Independence

It goes without saying that being independent is a strength. Being financially independent, taking care of ourselves and our homes, not being dependent on other humans to meet our every need—these are good things. But there is another side to the coin. As a recovering workaholic, I know what it is to push people away and insist on completing work on my own. It's not that I necessarily need the glory of finishing something on my own, but I need the personal satisfaction of knowing—of proving to myself—that I can complete something significant without help from others. I never really saw the downside of ultra-independence until the day I saw a meme on Jamila White's Instagram account that declared, "Sis, the inability to receive support from others is a trauma response." That stopped me in my tracks. Jamila's post explained that those of us with a tendency to push help away, to insist that we can do everything on our own, are using a survival tactic to try to shield our hearts from disappointment, betrayal, or neglect—the feelings that we previously experienced when others couldn't or didn't show up for us. Deep, right? Are you ultra-independent? Can you look back in your life to understand why?

I can still ask for and receive help;
it doesn't take away my independence.

• FEBRUARY 8 •

Liminal Space

I love the word *liminal*. It comes from the Latin word for threshold and refers to the state of being in between or poised between one stage and the next. For some reason, the idea of liminality has always conjured up a sense of possibility for me. It's that point between what is and what comes next. Although some people might interpret *liminal* negatively, since it kind of means uncertain, I prefer to spin it positively. Anything can happen, but I tell myself that something good or better comes out of liminal time and space. I'm probably making that up, but that's what works for me. When things are uncertain, I can tell myself I'm in liminal space, and *voilà*, I feel more hopeful. Apparently, that whole positive thinking thing works.

I rest and take deep breaths when I am
in a liminal space, knowing that whatever
comes next is in my best interest.

Loneliness

May Sarton once wrote, “Loneliness is the poverty of self; solitude is the richness of self.” I haven’t experienced loneliness for a long, long time. I know that I felt lonely growing up in my family and even lonelier in my phase of active addiction and dysfunction. I have certainly felt lonely in past relationships. Choosing recovery and finding out how much I love my own company has well cured me of loneliness, as has finding my people. My heart breaks for lonely people, especially for those in our recovery community who talk about feeling isolated and alone. I see and hear their pain, and I can remember what it was like. I can’t make anyone believe that if they just lean into community, they will find that one person or group of people who helps wipe loneliness from their lives. It takes trust to make connections. But it’s worth it.

Finding out how to be with myself was the first step to curing my loneliness.

Never Question Your Worthiness

Brené Brown says that we all deserve love and belonging, and that our worthiness is our birthright. Louder for the people in the back: *our worthiness is our birthright.* I love how solid, simple, and complete that phrase is. We don't have to prove our worthiness. We don't have to hustle or fight for it. We are worthy just through the simple act of being born.

Those of us in recovery need to work hard to stop questioning whether we are worthy or not of . . . anything. We deserve to be loved by our partner, our children, other family members, friends, and other important people in our life. We are worthy of forgiveness for what I like to call "the shit we did." We are worthy of respect and equality and health care and all the services we each need to heal. Don't question your worthiness, if you are still doing that. Just claim it.

Operating from a place of knowing we are worthy frees up a whole lot of time and energy.

Here to Listen

Author, inspirational speaker, and teacher Cheryl Strayed once said, "Compassion isn't about solutions." It's not easy to remember that. Or, rather, *I* find it difficult to remember that. When I'm listening to someone who is struggling or hurting, my first instinct is almost always to want to jump in with suggestions or answers to help ease or eradicate their pain. That's not compassion; that's not even active listening. So I try to bite my tongue and practice what I learned, when I did my recovery coach training, about listening compassionately. I try to stay silent, to pay close attention to the words that I am hearing as well as to the person's facial expressions, body language, and voice intonation. I listen for the silences between words. If invited to, I'm happy to pose questions that create a two-way dialogue, but again, I have to refrain from trying to fix what is going on for the person. Sometimes I need to say out loud to them, "I'm here. I'm listening." And then let them keep talking.

Cultivating compassion takes a lot of practice but very few words.

Self-Respect

We need to believe that we are worthy of respect if we expect other people to respect us. After all, we teach people how to treat us. Back in the day, I was always disrespecting myself. Naturally, I attracted disrespect on the regular. It took a long time in recovery to gain back my sense of self and then even longer to believe that who I had become deserved the respect of others—and of myself. I have come to know that self-respect may be a feeling or belief, but it's based in clear action. Sometimes it's cutting a person out of our life when they are disrespectful to us; other times it's walking away from a conversation that is disrespectful of another person or group of people.

There was a time I had zero self-respect. Now I attract respect. I have an overabundance of self-respect. For me, the quickest way to self-respect was to honor my word to myself, to keep my word to myself. Disrespect erodes everything. Self-respect restores—and attracts—more respect.

Do I show myself the respect I deserve?
Because I deserve to be respected.

Time Alone

It used to be that I couldn't bear to be by myself, and so I never was. Recovery changed everything. It took some time, but I can honestly say that today I am my very favorite person in the world to spend time with. I love my people, and I spend a lot of time with others, but I crave time that is just mine, to do as I please in the manner I please and at the pace that I want. At the very least, I make sure to be on my own for the first hour or so of every day.

Time alone is one of my non-negotiables. I know that when I feel overwhelmed, overstimulated, or anxious, I need to find solo time to replenish. When I'm irritable, have difficulty concentrating, or find myself tuning out the people I care about, it's because I need some renewal time. Trust me, everyone benefits when I turn off my world and the people in it and focus on "me" time.

Alone time feeds my soul, which could mean that I'm an introvert but more likely means that I love myself.

Intensity Is Not Intimacy

Once upon a time, I struggled with love addiction. The people I chose to love weren't very good for me, and even the ones who didn't do specific harm added little value to my life. The term *madly in love* fit for me when I was younger—everybody was always mad in my relationships. I found myself in addictive, unhealthy relationships because I confused intensity for intimacy. I know now that intimacy is about trust and reciprocity, authenticity, and emotional connection. Those words do not describe any of my early relationships.

My preference was to be in relationships that were intense, uncertain, and very dramatic. Some were high risk, and one was extremely violent. I was comfortable with intensity, and intimacy scared the hell out of me. I only learned what intimacy was, and how to create and participate in it in my life, when I started to establish nonromantic relationships with other people in recovery. I'm grateful every day for learning that intimacy heals and doesn't hurt.

My dearest friends in recovery have taught me what intimacy is and what it isn't.

Our Work Is Not Our Worth

I've long wondered why the most common question that we ask people when we meet them for the first time is "What do you do?" Is that the most important thing about them? I used to think that it was the most important thing about me. I still acknowledge and am proud of all the hard work that it took for me to get to where I am professionally. I do good work, and I believe that it's important, since it has focused on recovery. If you looked at my LinkedIn profile, you'd probably think I have a few good things going on. But the biggest lesson that I've learned in the last twenty years is that my work is not my worth. I don't hustle for my worthiness through my work anymore. I'm not saying that my work doesn't have value. It does. But I am not what I do. I'd rather people asked me "What do you love to do?" when we meet.

My work brings me great satisfaction and supports the life I want to lead, but it doesn't define me.

When We Give Too Much

You know how it feels when you see someone you love or care about struggle with a mental health or substance use issue? You personally want to help them, and you try your hardest to find the support they need or provide it to them yourself. That is a loving gesture. And sometimes it's also codependency. Sometimes that person isn't interested in receiving help, but you keep working hard at their recovery for them. It doesn't really work that way. It's important in cases like this that you focus on your own self-care and healing.

If you are a helper, healer, nurse, coach, or another type of health care or allied professional with a passion and drive to help others, you know that our soul-purpose work can also end up being something from which we ourselves need to recover. If we aren't mindful about how much we are giving away, we become fatigued at best, burned out or very ill at worst.

We can't give it all away, and we shouldn't.

If You Want to Write

I spent decades reading about writing before I took up writing as a regular practice. One of my favorite books on writing is Brenda Ueland's *If You Want to Write: A Book about Art, Independence and Spirit.* First published in 1938, this slim volume continues to inspire. Ueland's list of things that all of us who want to write need to know is instructive. You'll have to read the book to learn more, but the very best advice on writing I've ever received is Ueland's directive to "write freely, recklessly, in first drafts." She also reminds us to be "true, honest and untheoretical" in our writing. For someone with control issues who lives mostly in her head, writing freely and recklessly and untheoretically is a very tall order. I am sometimes paralyzed with perfectionism when I am trying to write; the words simply fail to come out, and when they do, they don't do a thing for me. But really, the moment I write words, I'm a writer, and it is healing. And I've learned to repeat over and over and over again as I write, "This is a first draft." As with recovery, just getting started, not perfection, is what counts.

If you want to write, place words on paper.
That is the project.

Words Unspoken

My parents never said "I love you" when my two brothers, sister, and I were growing up. I had a couple of aunts who said it to me, and I heard my favorite television parents Mike and Carol Brady say it all the time to their kids, but those words were unspoken in my childhood home. I was fifteen the first time my mom told me that she loved me. It was following my first accidental overdose on pills and alcohol, and I recall her saying, "You know we love you, right?" *Well, no, Mom, I haven't ever been too sure of that,* I remember thinking. But also, it meant everything to me. My mom didn't find it easier to say she loved me as the years went on, and my dad has only found those words since she passed away. But I'm okay. I now understand that my parents didn't depend on words to show us they loved us. They showed us in a thousand other ways, including showing up for me every time I needed them. When my mom passed away, I didn't feel like there were any words, of any nature, left unspoken.

Actions really do speak louder than words.

Emotional Sobriety

Emotional sobriety is something that all women in recovery should strive to achieve, regardless of what they are in recovery from. Quite simply, having emotional sobriety means having the ability to feel one's feelings. It's so much easier said than done for those of us who have spent years trying to run from, avoid, or numb out our feelings. Yet, our personal recovery is dependent upon our emotional healing. As Beverly Conyers notes in her book *The Recovering Heart: Emotional Sobriety for Women*, "Until we untangle the web of hurtful and damaging emotions that prevent us from seeing ourselves clearly, we will continue to suffer from our secret belief that something is wrong with us." Recognizing and then feeling the emotions that we have stored for so long takes great effort, and we don't have to do it alone. Importantly, there's no timeline or finish line for becoming emotionally sober. It's our life's work.

Wounded hearts do heal.

Being Forgiven

We don't get to determine when another person will be ready to forgive us, or if they ever will. Several years into my recovery, I decided that it was time to ask my mother to forgive me for something that I had done in my addiction that I knew had devastated her. Long story short, I had packed up my then-two-year-old daughter and moved over twelve hundred miles away from my parents without a word to them. My mom was shattered. Years later, she and I found our way back to each other tentatively, and I felt it was time to make an amends and ask for forgiveness. I went to her house, sat her down, and started to explain that I had something I needed to ask her forgiveness for. She looked me straight in the eye and calmly said, "You can apologize all you want, but if it's about the time you ran away to the Yukon with my granddaughter, save your breath. I can't forgive you for that." I was flabbergasted and simply replied, "Well, that is what this is about, so let's forget about it." And we did, for a while. About ten years later, when she was dying, she told me she forgave me.

We can't schedule when other people will be ready to forgive us.

Serenity Prayer

If you have been around recovery for a while, especially Twelve Step recovery, then you will be very familiar with the Serenity Prayer. If you aren't, google it! Two sisters who just happen to be incredibly dear friends of mine, and who facilitate meetings for Adult Children of Alcoholics & Dysfunctional Families (ACA), recently shared a revised version intended specifically for ACAs. It reads: "God (higher power) grant me the serenity to accept *the people* I cannot change, the courage to change *the one* I can, and the wisdom to know that one is *me*." How much simpler our lives would be if we could embrace and remember this simple prayer. I have wasted so many days of my life trying to change others; I'm just not willing to do that anymore. Wanting to change people today, I now understand, is related to me wanting to change my childhood and the way the people in it showed up for me. That's never going to happen, and I feel better having learned that. Does anything about this prayer resonate for you?

Higher power, please grant me the serenity to accept that I can't change other people or the past. That will save us all a lot of time and energy.

Intergenerational Trauma

Trauma is inherited, passed down from those who directly experience trauma to subsequent generations. I wish that my children could have been born into a family that had never experienced trauma, but that wasn't the case. When I made my way into the world, it was into a family that had, on both sides, a tendency toward red hair, great senses of humor, a little bit of musical and artistic talent, and some dysfunction and trauma. Because how we manage trauma can also be passed from one generation to the next, my parents managed it as theirs had, mostly by ignoring it. I don't judge my parents for not dealing with issues that, if resolved, might have changed my life and my siblings' lives. Nobody in that time knew that the trauma that took place in families could be similar to what my paternal grandfather and many of my uncles experienced as shell shock in World War II. When we know better, we do better. My parents did their best, and so have I. And so, too, will my children.

Trauma is passed on generation after generation; may you be supported to understand and deal with whatever trauma you may inherit.

The Next Generation

Because we are a mother-daughter team that started a women's recovery movement, my daughter and I talk often about what recovery will look like for the next generation of women in or seeking recovery. What we hope, with all sincerity, is that few women will need recovery, but we know that the opposite is probably true. The world is a complicated place these days, and the pandemic has worsened an already-serious mental health epidemic in the youth and young adult population. What we envision, and what our community and organization is holding, is that more young women will know that there is help to heal their lives. We older women have plenty of wisdom to share, but we are still learning too. We need to be joined by younger women if the modern women's recovery movement is to continue to thrive and grow. We need younger women's energy, their ideas, and importantly, their passion. It won't hurt to have their technological skills, either. I'm excited to see us grow in recovery, generations deep.

I'll be here, cheering us on in our recovery,
when I'm eighty. What a fun time that will be.

Connecting to Compassion

In her book *Befriending Your Body: A Self-Compassionate Approach to Freeing Yourself from Disordered Eating*, my friend Ann Saffi Biasetti offers an amazing perspective on compassion. Ann acknowledges that people in early recovery don't find it easy to feel self-compassion. When we embark on our healing journeys, we may not even know what compassion is, let alone feel worthy of giving it to ourselves. In these cases, Ann suggests, we can start by looking *outside* of ourselves to find compassion, and then *take it in*. She calls this "building compassion from the outside in." We can do this by acknowledging the people around us who care about us, or we can be inspired by a song that stirs compassion or books that focus on compassion. Connecting with these external sources of compassion and focusing on what is outside of us can, as Ann reminds us, awaken what is inside of us.

We can invite compassion into our lives,
embrace it, and then shower it upon ourselves.

The Law of Subtraction

Don't shun me, but I'm not really convinced that the law of attraction is as powerful as many of my friends think it is. The premise of that law is that positive thoughts bring positive results into a person's life. I don't disagree with that; I just worry that people embrace it and think that thoughts alone can change our lives. That's a rather privileged perspective. I think I'm more of a law of subtraction girl. The two laws are somewhat related. The law of subtraction basically says that if we want change in our lives, we must first create space for that change. This makes a lot of sense to me. I need to clear out the clutter to make room for things to come into my life. I subtracted drugs, love addiction, overwork (mostly), and various other things from my life years ago; these days it's all about subtracting self-doubt and fear. I'm ready for whatever the universe wants to bring me, but I'm also ready to go out and get it, rather than think it into being.

I'm not convinced that I can manifest
my desires with my thoughts, but thoughts
matter in what I can manifest.

Loving Our Inner Child

The year after I got serious about recovery, John Bradshaw published *Homecoming: Reclaiming and Healing Your Inner Child.* My therapist at the time recommended that I read it, and I did, and before I knew it everyone around me in recovery was reading it too. The premise of the book was that we each carry within us a wounded inner child who is seeking attention and healing. Our inner child's needs can be met when we learn how to reparent ourselves, to give ourselves what we didn't receive as children. It sounds complicated, but it works. The one thing that my inner child lacked most was knowledge that she was loved. Figuring that out was instrumental in my early recovery, and Bradshaw's work helped me give that little girl what she needed. I could close my eyes, picture little me, and tell her that she really was loved; her parents just didn't know how to show her love in a way that she would recognize. It was such a healing process, and I've continued to nurture little Dawn for these past many decades. Have you met your inner child and helped her process her past? Have you been able to show her that she has been worthy of love all along?

I see you, little one. I've got your back now,
and I had it then.

Switching Up the Questions

My sweet friend Katie and I were chatting recently about how intimidating the question "Who am I?" can be for women on a healing journey. Katie pondered aloud that maybe we are asking the wrong question. Rather than asking ourselves who we *are*, Katie suggested, we should ask ourselves, "What do I *want*?" Not "What do my kids, my partner, or my parents want?" Not "What does my boss or collaborator or friend want?" But simply "What do I want in my life and for my life?"

To get to those big questions, Katie suggests, we need to start asking ourselves what we want in each and every moment throughout each hour of the day. In a world where our default is to nurture and prioritize the wants of others, Katie's ideas remind us how sacred it is to allow ourselves the space and permission to ask ourselves what we want, and then sit in the silence to hear the answers that can only come from within. When we ask ourselves what we want, the answer needs to come to us as a full-bodied *yes* before we know that it is the answer we are seeking.

We can always find an answer to the question "What do I want?" We just need to create the time and the space to tap into it.

Recovery Rest Stops

Healing from trauma, addiction, mental or physical illness, or any other life issue is hard work. It can be truly exhausting. Do we get to take breaks? There are people in recovery who swear that once we are in recovery, we must *always* be working hard on it. There's even a saying that goes something like "If you're not working on recovery, you're working on a relapse." I'm not convinced that this is true. I view recovery as a lifelong journey, and I understand the importance of working on all the issues that arise as we heal and grow. But why shouldn't we rest and relax occasionally in our recovery? If we are feeling stable and doing well and have done the work we need to do to identify when we are feeling vulnerable, surely we can stop once in a while along our recovery journey and just enjoy the view. I don't think we should ever become overconfident, smug, or complacent in or about our recovery. But we can rest and replenish.

There's nothing wrong with stopping and
recognizing how far we have come,
and then sitting there a spell.

Sisters

Sisterly relations can be rather complicated, right? But I have loved my baby sister for longer than she has been on this earth. I remember being seven years old and desperately wanting a girl baby to come out of our mother's stomach—or wherever, made no difference to me. I already had two older brothers, but they never wanted to play house with me. The news came by phone after school: the baby had been born, it was a girl, and she was a leap year baby. I was so happy about the girl part but so incredibly worried about the leap year part. What I heard was that she was a "leper," which I didn't really understand, but I knew it was bad. Fortunately, somebody cleared that up for me right quickly. I'm so glad that I got my wish for a baby sister. We have traveled some rocky terrain together and apart, and we are both now in long-term recovery from many of the same things. We have shared amazing times together. As we both continue to heal, things get less complicated.

Having a sister is special. Having a sister who is also in recovery is a miracle.

MARCH

• MARCH 1 •

Connection

I received an email recently from a woman who had attended our first She Recovers conference back in 2017, in New York City. She wanted to let me know that she and three other women who had met each other for the first time there were still in contact nearly daily. Since that event, they had created their very own recovery support group over text. She talked about how they make deposits to and withdrawals from the group regularly and how amazing it felt to have people just outside the circle of their daily lives to lean on and to cheer for. The four women are in recovery from different things, mostly alcohol and drugs but also food, codependency, money struggles, relationships. They text funny stories about their lives, support each other through breakups, sing birthday songs to each other off-key in voice memos, and have shared pandemic struggles, mystery rashes, hot flashes, favorite songs, surgeries, lost jobs, and relapses. They have talked to each other on the precipice of a binge or right after a slip-up; they have even shared bedside texting and loving encouragement as one of them waited for a loved one to pass. This is the power of connection in recovery.

Never underestimate the importance
of female friendship in recovery.

• MARCH 2 •

Ready, Set, Stop

It's a recovering woman's prerogative to change her mind. (That's a universal law that I made up.) We can think we are ready for a social engagement, a trip, a job, a relationship, or a way of recovering, and then we can rethink just how ready we are. We can come to a full, hard stop, or we can take time to pause. We can take the time we need to reflect and, if necessary, switch directions. We can bail on commitments. We can break off relationships, cancel trips, and leave a support group. Changing our minds is a healthy practice.

Being comfortable with changing course is something that I've had to work on as I have grown in my recovery. I will always know when I need to revisit something if I trust my gut, listen to my intuition. I can find the courage to take action and do what is best for me, and I can let go of how changing my mind affects others. To thine own self be true. It works.

It's okay to change my mind. I usually know when something isn't right for me.

I Am Enough

Although my parents did the best they could, I did not often feel loved in my family and home. I grew up believing with everything in my core that I was not *enough*. It was a devastating feeling, and it nearly destroyed my life.

After a few years in recovery, I started to feel *nearly* enough, and I wanted more. Staying in recovery has brought me to a place of deep knowing that I am and always have been enough. Getting here took me learning how to let love in. It also took understanding that I *was* loved as a child; it just wasn't expressed in ways that I could see or feel. I'm able to feel my enough-ness now in large part because of the love that I have received from my dearest friends and mentors in recovery, and others who have loved my grown-up self.

We are all born *enough*, but it gets stripped away when we let others determine our worth. What I hope we all see in our recovery is that we can reclaim it. I don't have to be enough for anyone else but me.

We are all recovering from not-enough-ness.

The Space between Stories

I don't know about you, but in my family, my siblings and I tell very different stories about our childhood. It's as though we were raised by different parents in different households. Occasionally my heart breaks slightly when my sister talks about *her* mother, because *my* mother seems so very different. My memories of my mother are a little softer, gentler, maybe more accepting than my sister's. Still, she can own her truth and experience of our mother just as I have the right to own mine. She is eight years younger than I, so she really did have a different experience, and my mom was going through some hard things when I was no longer at home but my sister was. Somewhere between the stories we share about our mother is the story that my mother would tell if she were still alive. Despite the discomfort that our different perspectives sometimes create, my story, my sister's story, and my mother's presumed story are all richly woven together by deep love for one another, love that transcends time and fills the space between the stories.

Getting our childhood stories straight is less important than respecting one another's interpretations.

• MARCH 5 •

Decluttering Our Thoughts

Clutter isn't only those piles of belongings on floors or shelves that serve as barriers to comfort and serenity in your home. The clutter between my ears causes me the most stress: all those things that take up space that I really don't need anymore. My brain can be a messy place, an interesting place, and, without a doubt, an overcrowded place.

Thanks to therapy and mindfulness practice, I've learned how to pare down my thoughts. As I have made a practice of cleaning up my physical space, I can regard and contemplate the piles of thoughts that I've created in my head, decide what I need to keep and what I can throw away. Lately, I've been throwing out self-judgment and harshness. I've reorganized outdated ideas about what I need to be doing with my days and my life, scrapped fear and insecurity. Clearing out the negative mental clutter has created a lot more space for curiosity, positivity, and creativity.

How do you sort through your clutter? What are you making room for?

*I hang on to thoughts that serve
me well and chuck the rest.*

Self-Sabotage

Self-sabotage is a form of self-harm. We self-sabotage because we are afraid of failure; we feel undeserving of success or unworthy of going after or having good or even wonderful things. As author Alyce Cornyn-Selby wrote, "Self-sabotage is when we want something and then go about making sure it doesn't happen." Self-sabotage can show up in our work or our art, in our relationships or in those promises to ourselves that we just can't seem to keep. Some of the self-defeating behaviors that we employ as self-sabotage include procrastination, perfectionism, avoidance, self-medicating, disorganization, starting fights, micromanaging, negative self-talk, mindlessly scrolling through the internet, and even paralysis. The best cure for self-sabotage is to recognize our negative thoughts and replace them with positive ones, and then take small but consistent positive actions in the direction of our goals or dreams. Stopping any self-harming behavior that we've been engaging in for a long time is hard. But, as our friend and fellow recovering woman Glennon Doyle regularly reminds us (and it's also the name of her podcast), we can do hard things.

Believing that we are worthy and deserving of what we desire is half the battle.

Protecting Our Energy

Our personal energy field consists of the energy that flows through and around every one of us, interacting with all the systems of our mind, body, and spirit. The outer boundary of our individual energy field is sometimes described as a large oval-shaped cocoon that wraps around our body. Our body draws energy into itself from a universal energy field, and every single time we come into contact with another living being, we experience an energy exchange. Learning how to set boundaries to protect our energy is important, as our energy fields themselves can shift between porous and rigid. Avoiding or stepping away from activities or people that drain our energy can be helpful, but when that's not possible, using mindfulness to minimize our exposure to negativity can mitigate harm. It's best to move toward people and things that make us feel good, to spend time with those whose energy vibrations are high and inspire happiness. Other women in recovery are that type of people. Gravitate toward them.

Protecting our energy is crucial to our mental and physical health.

Peeling the Onion

Getting to the core of who I am and how I got to be me has been like peeling away the layers of an onion. From the moment I went to treatment for my substance use disorder at the age of twenty-seven, I have been shedding the skins that have both protected and hidden my true center. My layers, and yours too, are made up of experiences, thoughts, emotions, fears, love and love lost, and more. Some layers are tough to peel back; I know you know what I mean by that. I love the quote by author Nina Guilbeau, who wrote, "Like handling an onion, peeling off the 'husk' of our lives, sometimes makes us cry." I have shed many tears on the cutting board of my recovery. But I've also loved so much of what I've uncovered and reclaimed in the process of self-discovery—about myself, my past, my unique gifts, and my place in the world. I know that every year that I stay in self-exploration, I am getting closer to my core.

Life is made up of layering on things
and then peeling those layers away.

• MARCH 9 •

Our Soul's Purpose

I've been thinking lately about how our soul's purpose may be somewhat different from our life's purpose. I'm not sure exactly what I mean by that, but hear me out. When I think about my life's purpose, I think about things that I am meant to do in community, or in connection, or in relationship with others. My life's purpose might be to try to inspire women in recovery, or it might be to be the best darn grandmother I could ever be. My life's purpose might be to leave my family a little more healed from intergenerational trauma. On the other hand, my soul's purpose may just be to learn the meaning of rest, to embrace the softness I feel eludes me. My soul's purpose might be the opposite of doing something in my life. My soul's purpose may well be just . . . to be fully me.

Is there really any higher purpose
than simply being ourselves?

Financial Recovery

One of the first recovery-focused books I read that wasn't about substance use was Karen McCall's *Financial Recovery: Developing a Healthy Relationship with Money,* which I read when it came out in 2011. I had just hit the wall with workaholism and had chosen to give up two of my three careers. My immediate worries about doing that were, of course, financial. Never mind that if I had kept going, I might have lost my family and my health. It was a timely read. I've since learned that most of the women I know in recovery could benefit from paying some attention to financial recovery to confront self-defeating money behaviors such as overspending, chronic debt, no or low savings, and underearning—or the opposite, hoarding. As in other areas in which we choose to recover, finding our way to a healthier, more balanced relationship with our finances takes time and commitment. I'm still working through a few remaining financial recovery issues, but I'll tell you that so far, all the work I have completed has been well worth it.

The work of financial recovery is not finding and saving more money, although that's okay too. Financial recovery is about our relationship with money.

My Wish for You

I want you to know that my most sincere desire for you is simply that you know what hope feels like. And I hope you know, because we are both women in recovery, that I know your heart. I know how you felt the last time you did the thing you are trying not to do, even if it was just this morning. I know how great it feels when you prove to yourself you can stop, even if you can't stay stopped.

My wish for you is that you know you can be a nearly total fuckup for a large percentage of your life and still turn it all around and have a career you only dreamed of, or have babies if that is what you want, or even just raise the ones you have already. I wish for you that you get to go to school for a certificate or license or couple (or three) degrees, if that's what you want to do. And I hope that if you choose to be coupled, you find someone to live in partnership with who totally gets you, maybe even before you get yourself. I hope my wishes for you come true. You are so worthy.

What are your wishes for yourself in recovery?
May they come true.

Wanting What They Have

I think we can all relate to admiring personality traits that we see in other people, traits that we wish we had ourselves. For me, I think the thing I admire most in other women is their softness. When someone is calm, gentle, or soft-spoken, I naturally feel attracted to that in them. It's not that I'm hard, although I don't hesitate to admit that I have some hard edges. Somewhere along the way I developed a sarcastic streak, which I always intend to come off as majorly funny, but I think sometimes it comes off as harsh. Maybe not. Regardless, there's just something about softness that centers me. I know that my mother had both hard and soft edges; I suppose I could want more of who she was in my own life. I've written elsewhere that finding my softness is something I have left to do in this lifetime. I know that some people get softer with age. I hope I'm one of those people.

I won't give up on finding softness. I have plenty of time (I hope) to cultivate it.

Minding Our Mental Health

Mental health issues run in my family. Over the course of my life, I have been diagnosed with mild depression, melancholic depression (characterized by the inability to stop crying), and generalized anxiety. I have experienced and acted upon suicidal ideation, which is a symptom of, but not a diagnosis of, mental illness. I have experienced mental health issues both before recovery and in recovery. I still live with anxiety almost all of the time, but it is manageable. I consider myself one of the lucky ones. With the exception of the suicide attempts and melancholic depression (both of which occurred when I was in active addiction), my mental health conditions have been relatively mild. What I find fascinating about my mental health experiences is that I have always understood them to be biochemical, and I never hated myself for having them, at least not in the way I loathed myself for my addiction. I think if I were addicted today, I'd be encouraged by the way substance use issues are now often viewed as mental health matters. I'd feel less ashamed to seek help, at the very least.

Mental health matters. Mind yours.

• MARCH 14 •

Maybe We All Have It Right

I don't expect you, or anyone, to agree with all my ideas and opinions about recovery, all the time. For one thing, my ideas and opinions are ever-evolving, just as my own recovery is ever-changing. The main thing to keep in mind is that what I think about recovery almost always relates specifically to *my own recovery.* The only opinion of mine that I need you to agree with is that we all need to be supported to find and follow individualized pathways and patchworks of recovery. Period. That's it. And if we can agree upon that, there really isn't a whole hell of a lot of room for disagreement about recovery, right?

The thing about arguing over the "right" way to recover is that people's lives are at stake, especially if we are talking about recovering from mental illness, eating disorders, substance use disorders, and other addictions. We need more unity, more compassion, and more respect for multiple pathways if lives are to be saved. Can we all get together and make that a thing?

There is only one right way to recover.
And that is your way.

Find a Buddy (Anybuddy)

I strongly believe that having even just one friend in recovery is incredibly helpful to our recovery. Depending on what sort of recovery journey you are on, you may be familiar with the concept of having a "sponsor" or a "mentor" or maybe even just an "accountability buddy." All such relationships can be helpful. If you are in Twelve Step recovery, the pressure to "get a sponsor" can invite a lot of anxiety. You should take your time picking out someone to work the Steps with (which is the purpose of a having a sponsor). If you are in a different recovery community, you might think about asking someone with more experience to mentor you, or somebody with the same amount of experience as you to be your accountability buddy. I've seen miraculous things happen when women join forces to help each other stay the course. You should also know that you don't need to establish formal relationships if you aren't ready for a sponsor, mentor, or accountability buddy. Maybe just ask someone if you can text them once in a while or have coffee or go for a walk. The main point here is that everybody deserves a buddy in recovery. And I'm sure there is someone out there who would love to be yours.

There are other women out there looking
for the same level of connection as you are.
May you find each other.

Our First Obsession

Genetically, I believe that I was as predisposed to obsessive thought patterns and behaviors as I was to red hair and freckles. They're how I escaped, whether I thought I needed to . . . or just wanted to. The French concept of an *idée fixe* resonates for me—a dominant idea or thought, a desire or feeling, an obsession. Many of us in recovery can recall being obsessive as children. Some of us talk about escaping into food or video games. My obsessions were more around fantasies or make-believe, which on the other side can be seen as creative outlets, but I used them mostly to escape my reality. I used to obsessively fantasize about being adopted into a different family. I also escaped into reading the adventures of the Bobbsey Twins and Nancy Drew, and I had major fantasies around television. I wanted so desperately to be one of the kids on *The Brady Bunch* or *The Partridge Family*.

What were the earliest ways you chose to check out to escape or numb? How did your earlier behaviors reflect compulsive preoccupation? How do you manage your obsessions today?

Today, my biggest obsession is with living life.

Holding Healing Space

Being with another person's pain, allowing them to feel their pain and process it, is hard but rewarding. It's difficult to remember that we don't need to fix or save the person. We can just create the container, then sit in empathy, withholding judgment and advice. We can practice active listening, making sure our body language expresses compassion and patience. We should never interrupt tears.

But holding healing space is about more than being there for people in pain. We can hold space for the promise and joy of healing too. I've sat in circles of recovering women and witnessed their tears of pain turning into tears of awareness and gratitude. Affording someone the space and the grace to process what is true for them is one of the greatest honors in recovery. Witnessing a mental or emotional breakthrough, or in some cases even a spiritual awakening, is sometimes the reward for holding space. But we don't do it because we want anything back. We do it because other women hold and have held space for our healing too.

I hold space for other women's healing.
It's an honor and a privilege to do so.

The Magic of Us

My friend LeAnn suggests that the magic of people in recovery (the "us") comes down to our collective desire to tell the truth about ourselves and know the truth about each other. I think she's onto something. I want to know the real you as much as I need you to see and know the real me, with the caveat that in recovery, the most real versions of you and me are always going to be in flux.

In our community, we don't need to present as prettied up or watered down. We accept one another as we are in the flesh, in the fun and in the fury. We understand that our bodies are just containers for our untamed spirits and stories. We show up for one another clothed in our insecurities, wrapped in narratives rife with both trauma and triumph. The truth of who we are and who we are becoming is something to behold. But it's the witnessing, the being mirrors for each other as we heal and grow, that is the real magic.

Getting to know others helps me
to better know myself.

• MARCH 19 •

Anger as Our Friend and Teacher

A tweet by Canadian artist Lynds Gallant a few years ago changed how I think about anger. Gallant tweeted about her therapist's explanation that her anger was the part of her that knew the abuse and mistreatment Gallant had experienced was unacceptable; her anger was the part of her that loved her and knew that she deserved to be treated kindly. Gallant went on to reflect that her anger is her brain's way of shouting "This isn't okay!" I had never thought about anger in that light, but it makes sense. Inspired by the tweet, now when I get angry, I ask myself what my anger is trying to tell me. Often the anger is signaling that something related to what I am angry about is not just or right. Sometimes it's about past wrongs that are being triggered; other times it's about current injustices or perceived injustices. What I know today is that I can befriend my anger, learn something from it, and let it go once it has done its job. Anger has a purpose in recovery; we just need to figure out what it is for each of us.

When we view anger as a part of us that loves us,
we can let it guide us and then let it go.

Holding Tight

There are two sides to holding tight. First, there's holding tight to hope, holding tight to our values, holding tight to our recovery, holding tight to those we love. These are all positive. Hope is sometimes the thing we need most, and our ideals and values are always worth holding on to tightly. Holding loved ones close feeds our hearts like few other things can.

There is another side of holding tight, and it's not nearly as good for us. Sometimes we hold on so tight to someone that we smother them, or at the very least fail to give them the space they need to be themselves or grow on their own. We can hold on so tightly to a resentment that it colors every other area of our life with misery. Do you have any experience with that? Some of us also hold tightly to stories that no longer serve us and behaviors that harm us. What are you holding on to today that is supporting your wellness? What do you need to release your grip on to continue to grow?

Hold on tightly to that which serves you
and release the things that don't.

• MARCH 21 •

Life Is Good in Recovery

Today, I like myself, almost all the time. I have healthy, happy people in my life; I keep the unhealthy ones whom I can't remove from my life on the periphery, where I can love them from afar. I've learned how to accept them for where and who they are, not try to change them. I'm not a perfect partner, mother, grandmother, daughter, sister, or friend, but I'm pretty good, and all relevant parties know that I love them with my whole heart and that I am always trying. They know because I tell them that I love them all the time, and I admit to them when I feel I am falling short. I give myself grace when I don't meet my own standards. I like to think that life is always good and never bad, but I also know that it can be truly great at times as well. Life is a spectrum of goodness in recovery. I'll take it.

From good to great—that's how
I choose to view my life.

Imposter Syndrome

It has taken me many decades, plenty of therapy, and a lot of practice, but I have finally gotten a handle on my imposter syndrome. I usually only experience it at conferences when I'm surrounded by highly educated people. Even though I have a PhD, I can feel like I don't really belong among the "brainiacs" most of the time. The syndrome, which is regularly experienced by even the highest-functioning people among us, is characterized by feelings of self-doubt and personal incompetence as well as a sense that any personal success is due to luck rather than skill, education, or experience. Even the renowned author Maya Angelou struggled with imposter syndrome, writing, "I have written eleven books, but each time I think, 'Uh oh, they're going to find out now. I've run a game on everybody and they're going to find me out.'" For just a moment, writing the above, I had a moment of thinking I'm an imposter for thinking that I have the same right to claim the syndrome as Maya Angelou. Now that's a little bit messed up, right?

I don't have to be the smartest person in the room to admit that I'm smart too.

• MARCH 23 •

Hiding in Humor

One of the first things I explored in psychotherapy during my early recovery was my tendency to always use humor when I brought up painful things that had happened or were happening in my life. I couldn't seem to *not* make a joke when discussing sensitive issues. It was disheartening to feel—at first—like that was a *bad* thing. I really preferred to think that my life was just unusually amusing. My therapist helped me to understand that, although using humor was the way I deflected or postponed feeling discomfort and pain, I didn't need to judge my doing so as a bad thing. It was, she helped me to understand, a coping mechanism. I just needed to recognize it for what it was—a delay tactic. Today, I try not to hide in humor when I'm processing hard things, but old habits die hard. I take note when I make something painful out to be funny and remind myself that I need to dig a little deeper and get to the real feelings beneath the matter.

Making light of heavy things in my life
is a protective reflex; it's okay for laughter
to precede tears.

• MARCH 24 •

Moving beyond Recovery Silos

When I first landed in recovery, I needed help for many things, including my addiction to drugs and unhealthy relationships, my anxiety, and my codependency. I needed to learn how to live substance-free, but I also needed to understand how being raised in a dysfunctional family and subsequent traumas had shaped my existence. There just weren't enough days in the week for me to attend all the support meetings that I needed, and even if there had been, as a newly single mother on welfare, I couldn't have afforded the babysitting bill. So I started with a Twelve Step program that promised me relief from my drug addiction. It helped somewhat, until the other things that I needed to address would pop up, and I would use drugs. I look back and wonder if early recovery would have been easier if I'd found a place where I could have brought *all* of me to recover. A place where I could bring my co-occurring disorders, my love addiction, and the trauma that lay under it all. I'm sorry that place didn't exist for me back in the day, but I'm delighted that it exists today. It's called the She Recovers movement, and I am proud to have been a part of creating it.

You don't have to compartmentalize the things you are in recovery from anymore.

• MARCH 25 •

Addiction

Dr. Daniel Sumrok says that addiction shouldn't be called addiction, that it should be called "ritualized compulsive comfort-seeking." That speaks to my experience relative to my drug addiction and my work addiction—both things were spurred on by my needing to find comfort for unhealed trauma and anxiety. Although I've managed to quell a lot of the more destructive addictive behaviors in my life, I still have addictive tendencies, and those tendencies are still closely tied to anxiety. My iPhone gives me regular reports on how long I spend comfort-seeking on that device, which may not be destructive, but it sure does a lot to impede productivity. I drink hot cups of sweet tea compulsively throughout most days, but I don't want to assign any negative connotations to that ritual—so I won't. Still, thinking of addiction in the way that Dr. Sumrok suggests is both provocative and affirming.

I'm grateful to live at a time when people are open to new ways of thinking about addiction.

Codependency

There appear to be a great many definitions of *codependency* nowadays, but when I first got into recovery thirty-some years ago, the label *codependent* was largely reserved for people who were related to or in a romantic relationship with someone who was addicted to alcohol or drugs. The understanding of what constitutes codependency has broadened, and one no longer has to be closely connected to someone with a dependency problem to qualify. In the past, I have qualified as codependent. What that looked like was having a difficult time identifying my own needs in a relationship but being hyper-focused on what the other person needed. I was a people pleaser. I got swept up into other people's dramas at the expense of my own energy and well-being. It looked like me working harder to resolve a person's issues than they did. My codependency was present when I lacked the ability to recognize boundaries set by others and could not set my own, when I got lost in other people and could not find myself. If any of this resonates for you, don't panic. Take a deep breath. There is help, and you can recover.

Healing from codependency requires me
to put myself first, no matter how
uncomfortable that feels.

Digital Detox

The fact that our smartphones have taken over our lives makes me wonder just how smart we are. Okay, I'll speak for myself. On a scale of 1 to 10 indicating how addicted to my smartphone I am, I am probably a 7 most days. Fortunately, there are ways to moderate our phone attachment, and I think we would do well to try one or more of them occasionally. In *Off: Your Digital Detox for a Better Life,* Tanya Goodin provides a wealth of ideas for un-numbing from our devices. For example, she suggests that we can, in no particular order, put our phone on mute so we aren't constantly overstimulated by notifications; not take our phone into the bathroom; not have our phone in front of us when we are eating; not take our phone into our bedroom. In addition to setting these various boundaries, Tanya says that we can also keep our hands and brains busy with other things, such as coloring, doing a puzzle, reading, and another of my favorite pastimes, writing. I choose to moderate my phone usage primarily by putting my phone in a different room throughout the day and not taking it to bed. What are you willing to try?

Turning off and tuning out of our phones
can breathe new life into our days.

• MARCH 28 •

Giving Up Gossip

Yuck. Gossip. When we're young girls, gossiping is somehow one of our favorite pastimes, and when we land in a new group or community, it might still be one of the ways in which we try to bond with others. We may not even know the difference between gossiping and just talking about other women in recovery. So how do we distinguish between healthy conversation and gossip? Gossip is usually spread behind a person's back, and if the person being talked about knew that she was being talked about, she would likely be hurt. Pretty strong indicators between right and wrong, yes? One of the many things that amazes me about the women's recovery communities that I belong to is that there is an almost complete absence of gossip. I attribute this to the fact that each one of us is focused on healing ourselves, and we are more sensitive and attuned to negative energy when talking about others. It feels crappy, so we don't do it. I'm not saying we are perfect, but in general we are really dialed in to our personal growth and development, so we think twice about what we say about people and how it might impact them.

Keep the energy fields of recovery clear and kind.
Gossip has no place in recovery.

Caring for Our Physical Selves

One of the most important things I have figured out in recovery is that taking care of my body is good for more than just my physical health; it improves my psychological, emotional, and spiritual health. Importantly, I've also had to learn that caring for my body is not about changing my body; I accept my shape and my weight and no longer waste time wishing that either were different. These days, I focus on things that make me feel better in my body. I try to get enough sleep at night, but I am also really into naps. I move my body—usually slowly—but I also like to get my heart rate up. I eat foods that make me feel good, but I no longer subscribe to the belief that food itself can be good or bad. I hydrate. And I follow a maintenance plan not unlike the one my car is on, with annual checkups, regular dental and eye examinations, mammograms, and even colonoscopies (because I had colon cancer that one time). I am not a master at physical health care, but one day at a time, I do my best. What do you do for your physical self-care?

Daily attention to the container that holds my life matters; so far, it's running pretty well.

Depression

When I hit one of my last bottoms with substance use, I landed in the hospital, where I proceeded to cry for a solid three days. People around me from my Twelve Step program claimed that it was just Step One, which meant I was powerless over my addiction and my life had become unmanageable. Fair enough, but I was also clinically diagnosed with melancholic depression, a condition characterized by persistent and intense feelings of sadness and hopelessness. It all described me perfectly.

Depression is about brain chemistry; it's clinical. Depression is common, but everyone's depression is unique. When I'm clinically depressed, it affects my mood, my thoughts, my behavior, my ability to eat and take care of myself. I no longer cry when I'm depressed; I just exist in gray fuzziness. I'm fortunate that the depressive episodes I've experienced in recent years haven't taken me into the black holes of depression that I experienced in the past and have watched so many of my close friends experience recently. I'm grateful that I understand my particular experience of depression and that I can manage it when it visits.

Chemicals affect us all, whether they are substances we ingest or the chemicals that determine how our brains and bodies work.

• MARCH 31 •

Soul Sisters

I have an amazing sister, and quite miraculously, we are both in recovery. She will always be my number one sister. However, we don't have to share DNA to connect with other women as soul sisters. There is something beyond special about the relationships that we create with like-hearted women in recovery. I attribute the closeness that I find in my many recovery relationships to a shared understanding of what pain and struggle feel like—we connect on that spiritual level. But it's also easy to get close because in the recovery circles that I frequent, we bypass the small talk and dive right into the meaningful stuff. It's not uncommon for opening conversations to go something like this: "Hey, great to meet you. How is your day going?" Common responses might go something like this: "Pretty good, other than my post-traumatic stress disorder was triggered earlier today." I mean, we get that deep that quick. We connect on experience, intellect, and the ways that we recover the same or differently, but most of all, we connect deep in our souls. I'm not saying that those connections happen 100 percent of the time for women, but in my experience, it's been a solid 90 percent.

When women in recovery ask you how you are doing, they don't want to hear that you are fine. Dig deeper and share your true self.

APRIL

• APRIL 1 •

Don't Settle

I was nearly thirty years old when I figured out that I was worth more than I had been settling for in multiple areas of my life. Embracing the idea that I was deserving of more was easier than acting on that idea. I had to practice walking away from things that were not serving my highest good. Looking back, I mostly settled because I didn't think I was worthy of having more, but sometimes I settled because it felt easier or more comfortable. Sometimes, I settled because I was afraid to make waves by changing or leaving.

We are always cutting ourselves short when we settle. We don't have to settle in our relationships (romantic or otherwise), in jobs that don't work for us, or on recovery pathways that don't align with our values. The opposite of settling is choosing. When we stop settling and only accept or choose what we deserve, we take back our self-respect and find it easier to practice integrity.

We set our standards high when we remember our worth.

• APRIL 2 •

Stay above the Fray

Don't allow other people to steal your serenity. Just living our lives means that we'll find ourselves in plenty of stress-inducing and toxic situations that are not of our own making. Let's face it: people don't always present as the best versions of themselves. I believe that the old saying "Not my circus, not my monkeys" should be employed at every opportunity.

I receive a lot of invitations to engage in other people's turmoil. The trick, I've found, is to decline such invitations clearly and deliberately. Sometimes I speak with my body and leave a setting that is fraught with negative energy. When I can't physically leave or there is some value to my staying, I can use my words to draw a boundary around myself. I can say, "I am staying out of what is happening here, because I don't have the energy it would take to get drawn into it." Full stop. I can observe the situation without engaging. The trick is to listen to the noise without contributing to it and try not to get hooked into it emotionally.

Staying out of other people's bedlam
takes practice. But I can do it.

• APRIL 3 •

Taking a Me-Tour

My new friend Leena posted something in a WhatsApp chat a while ago that struck me as slightly brilliant. She was talking about being on her way home from one of our summer retreats, filled with ideas and lists of things that she needed to do, when she decided to take a "me-tour." Think *detour,* but more of a diversion for our soul. Leena found a spot to plant herself, took some time to sit by water, journaled a bit, and soaked up a beautiful sunset. It wasn't a huge detour—she did make her way home shortly thereafter—but she was filled up with both the regulating experience of the me-tour and the pride she felt for making herself a priority. I think everybody should think about taking more me-tours. During our regular day-to-day lives, most of us are annoyed when we are forced to take a detour, but choosing to take a me-tour sounds totally replenishing. What might your me-tour look like?

We can switch up our routes to and from home or work, and in so doing find a little bit of time to feed our soul.

Clearing Physical Clutter

As a person in recovery from anxiety, I find that household or workplace clutter can be highly problematic for me. It's automatic: I see disorder, I feel disordered. However, as a person also in recovery from perfectionism, I have had to train myself to live and work with at least some clutter around me. It's a tricky balance.

I'm fortunate that my tiny, crooked little old house has an extra room where I can hide the overflow of my life. As they say, "Out of sight, out of [anxious] mind." Our upstairs guest room usually looks like somebody's life has exploded in it. As in, my life has usually exploded in it. I only sort out the massive mess if company comes to stay. And I always feel very accomplished about it. Because I am a recovering workaholic and place such high value on my work, my home office gets more regular attention than other spaces in the house. I work in piles. Neat piles, but plenty of them. It's what works for me. What works for you?

The spaces that I live and work in don't need to be perfect for me to live or work in them.

• APRIL 5 •

Simple Things

Life was very complicated for me at one point, which is why I am so drawn to the simplest things today. The word *simple* means "easily understood and done." It took me a while, but I understand simple now, and I do it quite well most days. It doesn't mean I don't add things to my life; I just add them in an intentional way. Several years ago, I bought myself a milk frother so I could enjoy a creamy coffee or tea latte whenever I liked. It still brings me the greatest joy. I love reading and buy a lot of books but also treasure my trips to the public library. Having a novel on the go every day of my life is simple but entirely satisfying. A sunrise, a sunset, flannel pajamas, a puzzle (but not over one thousand pieces), playing with my little grandkids, or lighting a fire in the fireplace—these things fill me up more than any grandiose plans or projects ever could. Laura Ingalls Wilder said, "It is the sweet, simple things of life which are the real ones after all." I can't argue with that. How do you do simple?

I'm grateful for the simple things that
I've learned to love in recovery.

• APRIL 6 •

I See You

Hey, friend. I know that you have a hard time sharing the pain that was your past, but I want you to know that I know it still exists for you. I don't need to know the details around what wounded you so deeply to acknowledge that you were harmed. I respect that you let things out and invite people in cautiously, and that is how it should be. We get to set the schedule for how our healing unfolds. Our timeline. Our parameters. I see your strength and sometimes wish that you could embrace the opposite of strength, only so that you could feel the support of those of us who love you and who are here to hold you through the leaning into pain. I honor the work that you do—the journaling, the creating, the handiwork—that allows you to drop feelings and hopes and dreams down on paper as art. You are a person who shows up for everyone else in your life, always, even when we are messy and emotional and bleeding feelings all over the place. I know you will bleed, too, when you are ready. We'll be here with all the emotional first aid you might need.

Friends accept that friends will feel
out loud when they are ready.

• APRIL 7 •

What We Inherit

I inherited a lot from my mother. I inherited her love of reading novels and watching old movies and savoring hot cups of sweet tea. Like her, I think everything is better with butter on it, and while we both loved travel, home is always where we both fit best. I inherited none of my mother's passion or skills related to cooking or baking, but I have some of her jewelry and most of her book-of-the-month-club books. I inherited her intelligence and her warmth, her love of family and of family history.

Although I know that she never wanted me to, I also inherited my mom's trauma. Her childhood wounds closed her off emotionally for much of my life, to my great detriment. I am grateful that my recovery prompted conversations between us that led to some healing for her, some answers for me. She passed heartbreaking stories on to me that I still hold, but not too tightly. I do my own work to release them. Showing me that it's never too late to open and change was perhaps the greatest gift that my mother could ever leave me.

Sometimes the most valuable heirlooms
we inherit are lessons on life and love.

• APRIL 8 •

Second Chances and More

Everyone who needs recovery deserves as many chances as it takes to get grounded in a recovery journey. It takes what it takes. As wearisome as it might be for those who love or care about us, I hope they know that they can't give up on us. We'll get there.

I was privileged to be given so many chances to recover in my past, but some opportunities just came before I was ready. I don't ever take lightly the fact that many people aren't as fortunate as me. They don't have people, as I did, who are supremely patient with them. Or else the risks they take are such that their life is taken and, with it, any chance they may have had to recover. I do recovery for me and for the people who care about me, but I also recover in honor of the people I know who've lost their lives and any chance to recover. I do what I do because they cannot, and I'm nearly certain that they wish they could have.

As tired as we or others may be of us,
we always deserve a second chance.

Belonging

I feel sad admitting that I don't remember feeling like I belonged in my family when I was young. I'm not quite sure why that was. I fantasized about living with various other families; some were relatives, others were friends. When I was a teenager, I was smart, but I didn't feel like I belonged with the smart kids. I wasn't cool enough to be a part of the cool kids' group, and I was a little bit afraid to hang out with the misfits, although that's probably where I fit best. When I fell into drug addiction, I finally found a place that felt like it was mine, with people who got me and whom I understood. This was unfortunate; it was dangerous, but it was the truth. When I landed in recovery, I again felt like I fit almost immediately with the women who had been where I had been, done the things that I had done. I've never lost that sense of belonging in recovery, and I feel at home in any and just about all recovery spaces that have women in them. But most of all, I feel that I do belong in my family of origin now, as well as in the family that I have created myself.

I had a longing for belonging,
and now I truly belong.

Cultivating a Space of Our Own

The older I get, the more value I place on creating spaces where I can just be and hang out alone. I am incredibly privileged to live in a lovely, crooked little old house that has a lower level I have turned into my very own She Cave. Every piece of furniture, each household amenity, and all the décor was lovingly chosen and placed by me. Memories and markers of my full and simple life are everywhere, as are books, tarot decks, candles, and comfy blankets. My favorite colors, pale turquoise and chocolate brown, are celebrated throughout as accents. I know that not everyone has such a richness of space to herself, and I don't take it for granted. But I'm proud of the life that I have built, even fought for, in recovery. One of the biggest gifts that I've received in recovery is to feel comfortable in my own skin, in my own company. I celebrate that in my own space every day.

Perhaps not today, but one day I hope that you, too, can create a sacred space for yourself.

• APRIL 11 •

Finding Congruence

For as long as I can remember, I have had trouble remembering the words *congruent* or *congruence* or *congruency* when I most need them to make a point in conversation. I know the words and I attach great meaning to them; I just happen to lose them when I'm looking for them. When two things are congruent, they are harmonious, in agreement, compatible. For a long time, including not that long ago, my life was incongruent. It didn't work. I think that's why I have a mental block about the concept. In active addiction, I did not want to be the person I was being; I didn't want to be killing myself with drugs. When I was at the height of my workaholism, I didn't want to always be abandoning my family and friends in favor of work. Both are examples of not being congruent. When I am speaking with a woman who is agonizingly unhappy about how she is showing up in her life, I know the word that I need to pull out to help her. I just can't usually seem to find it. It's a quandary. And maybe an irony.

Recovery will support you to live your life in congruence with your values and desires. Embrace that.

Things Left to Do

I have a few important things to take care of before my life ends, which I hope and assume won't happen for a long while. The list is not unmanageable. I have a few books and a screenplay to write. I need to reread a bookcase full of my favorite novels. I need to visit Greece and Italy for the first time, and I need to take a few big family vacations. I need to take many road trips across the beautiful island that we call home and catch many more sunrises and sunsets at the beach. I have to go through all my journals and diaries and probably tear out a page or two. I need to make lists of who gets my jewelry and books, and write letters to leave for my kids and grandkids. And I need to do that thing I've promised myself I would do for the past three decades of recovery, which is to establish a more consistent meditation practice. Perhaps I should start with that. I think it might help nail in all the other things. What's on your to-do list?

We shouldn't wait to start crossing things off our life's to-do list.

Writing Our Recovery

I write for a living, but what I get paid for is professional and academic-style writing. I love it, and it's important work because most of it focuses on women, mental health, addiction, and recovery. But it's *this* kind of writing, sharing here what I have learned and experienced in my life and in my recovery, *this* is the type of writing that drives me to my computer most days. Although I'm usually jazzed to share my thoughts about recovery (I have at least 366 thoughts, apparently), I also like to keep a lot of my writing private. I cannot tell you how many (partially filled) journals I have, many of them with tear stains on the pages. I bleed all over the paper (not literally, and besides, I type more now). My rawest writing is the writing where I try to process what the hell is going on for me. The kind of writing that allows me to get in touch with myself on such a deep level that I scream or laugh or cry so hard for my dead mother that snot drips onto my keyboard. If you haven't tried writing your recovery, I highly recommend it. Doesn't it sound fun?

Some of what we write is meant for each other,
and some for our very own hearts.
Both are beautiful.

Disappointing Others

Learning the art of saying no to other people wasn't easy. I used to always come up with extravagant stories, excuses, or narratives for why I couldn't do something. Nobody ever taught me that I could just simply say no. I grew up believing that somehow saying no to others would do them harm. I didn't understand that saying yes sometimes causes myself harm. Like my friend Holly Whitaker says, "Disappoint other people with your no; don't disappoint yourself with a yes you'll later resent." Isn't that the truth?

There's such freedom in saying no. Perhaps you know this. I'm a recovering people pleaser, so it took me a little longer than most to figure this out. I'm really good at it now. When we say no to other people, we don't need to overexplain, lie, manipulate, justify, or make excuses. We can decline graciously, confidently, firmly. We don't *need* to justify our decisions. We can respond with a simple "Thanks for thinking of me, but I'm going to pass" or "Sorry, I'm unavailable for that" or even better, "No, thank you." If you don't already do this, try it out.

I'd rather disappoint others than
disappoint myself.

From the Extreme to the Ordinary

In my teens and throughout my twenties, everything about my life was on a spectrum of extremes. I went from being emotionally neglected to anxious, from confused to abused, from numbed out to strung out, from traumatized to depressed and suicidal. That I survived living a life of such extreme chaos and pain is slightly miraculous. I have no difficulty finding gratitude for my life today. And what blows me away now is that I have no desire whatsoever to live on the extreme end of anything these days. I can handle a little bit of anxiety and confusion, but that's the extent of it. I'm not comfortable numbing out (although I can still do it sometimes), and I have zero tolerance for abuse, whether self-inflicted or from outside of myself. I haven't thought about ending my life since I found recovery. What I am drawn to most these days is living an ordinary life. Simple. Calm. Happy. Extremely ordinary is all that I can handle today.

If there are degrees of ordinary,
I'm here for all of them.

Making Meetings

I strongly believe that attending groups or gatherings or meetings with other recovering women is a wonderful way to get connected to your new way of life and to other women who are seeking healing. There are so many platforms and programs, you can attend meetings regularly—for free. As with most things, I always suggest that you try different options until you find the one that fits. And then I recommend that you attend meetings as regularly as you can. In some corners of the recovery world, it's suggested that you attend ninety meetings in ninety days to establish a recovery foundation. If you are a single person without any other commitments (job, family, pets), that is something you might consider, but I have always thought that "ninety in ninety" is much too high a bar to set for most of us. I'd rather suggest ninety days of self-care with as many meetings as you think you can manage after you have found time to do the things that you already know help your recovery (walks, creative pursuits, naps) and after you have worked, taken care of other loved ones, gone to therapy, etc. How many meetings you attend is your business. Nobody else's.

Make room for as many recovery meetings
as fill you up, but not so many
that they drain you.

• APRIL 17 •

They Are One of Us

Over the past several years, I have had the incredible honor of sitting on a She Recovers conference stage and interviewing famous women who identify as being in recovery from something or other. Glennon Doyle. Elizabeth Vargas. Janet Mock. Ashley Judd. In each instance, I was petrified—petrified that I would freeze or say something dumb and alienate them, scared that they would see my insecurity and judge me to be a fraudulent specimen in recovery. Neither of these things happened. Rather, these extraordinary women in recovery reminded me, once we got to talking, that we are all more alike than different. They reminded me that our stories of healing from bulimia, addiction, anxiety, childhood neglect and abuse, mental health issues, or sexual assault are common threads of experience that stitch us together and place us all on a level living field. When women who are in the public eye tell their recovery stories, as these celebrities do, they help break down the stigma for all of us. May even more speak up—we need them now more than ever.

Differences matter, but they fall away
for a time when we share our recovery
stories from the heart.

• APRIL 18 •

Self-Validation

As individuals, we get to determine what our personal successes look like. Unfortunately, we are used to allowing *others* to tell us what success looks like. We become so used to looking for validation from others that we lack the clarity we need to even assess how well we are doing. For example, the great job that we get is only great if the people in our life think it's great, or that wonderful thing we did for somebody else is only of value when other people remark on how wonderful it is. This is not a fun or healthy way to exist. Each one of us must determine what our success will look and feel like; we are our own barometers of what hits the mark for us as individuals. We must each be in control of our own recovery.

The good news is that becoming stronger at self-validation becomes easier when we think about what success will look like in advance. Committing to yourself that you will remain sober for one week at a time, and then doing that, is a success. It will also give you the confidence you need to keep moving forward. Celebrate your successes, always.

Validating what success looks like for us
is about recapturing our own agency
over ourselves and our recovery.

Our Story Can Change in an Instant

One Saturday evening in April 2022, I sat in an audience of five hundred women in recovery listening to the remarkably lovely Ashley Judd share about her journey to spiritual wellness. She spoke to many aspects of her growth as an adult child of dysfunction, referring several times to her healed relationship with her beloved mother, Naomi Judd. On that warm night in Miami, Ashley talked about knowing how to "be together" with her mom and about their deep love and affection for one another. She spoke to us about finding understanding, acceptance, and forgiveness in their relationship.

Seven days later, Ashley and her sister, Wynonna, announced that their mother had passed away after years of suffering from mental illness. And just like that, Ashley's and Wynonna's own lives and stories were forever changed. The same is true for all of us: deep loss transforms our recovery stories, especially when the most important characters in that story leave us. Fortunately for us, the loving, healing parts of our stories are embedded in our souls and live on forever.

Our stories are not static; they grow and change with every heartbreak.

• APRIL 20 •

Embracing Confusion

Do you ever feel so lost, stuck, and confused about a situation that you don't know what to think or do? Me too. It's not a comfortable place to be, but I've learned that confusion can't be ignored; it needs to be embraced to get to the other side of it. We have to admit to ourselves that we don't have an easy answer to whatever it is that is confusing the hell out of us. And then, we need to start working through the confusion. Gently. That can mean writing about the situation, literally freestyling and dropping thoughts onto paper, not trying to make sense of any of the words. That might help us get comfortable enough to speak our confusion aloud to another person. Perhaps a close friend will give us some time and listen to us as we process the wide array of conflicting thoughts and ideas. It's good to remind that friend that we don't need them to find a solution to our confusion; we need them to be there while we work through to the other side. And we will get to the other side, as long as we cultivate curiosity and ask ourselves the right questions.

Are you confounded and confused about anything in your life today? Embrace it.

Unplugging

Author and woman in long-term recovery Anne Lamott is credited with the brilliant saying "Almost everything will work again if you unplug it for a few minutes, including you." And yet, unplugging is the last thing that many of us are willing to do. Nearly half of the respondents in a recent survey admitted to spending an average of five to six hours on their phone each day, and that didn't include work-related time. Another quarter of respondents spent three to four hours on their phone daily. Lamott's advice to unplug for a few minutes is wise, but in my own life I've had to revise it to unplug for a few hours, rather than minutes. I play a lot of games with myself around my phone use, but it is very obvious that my anxiety is lessened and I am much more present to myself and others on the days when I put my phone away for a few hours. Unplugging for a few minutes doesn't really cut it for me these days. How about you? Can you unplug for hours? If not, can you practice unplugging for fifteen, thirty, or forty-five minutes at a time? What feelings come up when you do that? What helps you unplug?

Unplug and live.

• APRIL 22 •

She Time

I have learned a lot about how to organize successful women's retreats over the years, but the biggest thing I have learned is that anybody can host or plan a retreat. Retreats don't require travel to distant places or private chefs. All you need is a weekend on the calendar and a house; a vacation rental can work wonders, and if split between six to eight participants, it can be quite inexpensive for some. The packing list is simple: books, cozy clothes and pajamas, toiletries, walking shoes for outside, slippers for indoors. A deck or two of tarot cards is always encouraged, and a journal to capture the magic of what unfolds is highly recommended. The connection, the laughter, and even the tears are what make women's retreats memorable, but food is also a key element. Potluck is always the way to go. The pace for the weekend should be set at slow. Naps are delicious. A little yoga or a hike can be nice, as can sitting around a campfire, if available. Guitars are welcome; good singing voices optional. I wish you all at least one retreat per year. You are beyond worthy.

A women's retreat is a
pajama party for adults.

• APRIL 23 •

Releasing Our Shortcomings

I love the program and the underlying principles of Twelve Step recovery, but the language about dealing with our defects or shortcomings stopped working for me years ago. I no longer use the term *defect* to refer to any aspect of myself because I no longer believe that I am defective (although I did, for way too long). The term *shortcoming* is easier to digest, as I do have a few negative patterns in my life that I need some help with. I'm drawn to something that I learned in a book by Thérèse Jacobs-Stewart called *Mindfulness and the Twelve Steps.* Writing about the Seventh Step, which is about asking for our shortcomings to be removed, Jacobs-Stewart introduces a Buddhist-inspired aspiration practice that supports us to walk in the direction of desired change. Using mindful meditation, we set an intention or make a vow to let go of what no longer serves us and open our heart to having it replaced with something new. If we have a higher power (I do), we can ask for help to take action to follow through. It works.

There's a lot to be said about
being willing to change.

• APRIL 24 •

Blooming in Recovery

One of my favorite quotes is "And the day came when the risk to remain tight in a bud was more painful than the risk it took to blossom."* It nearly brings me to tears as I sit here, thinking about how it feels to regularly witness women blooming in recovery. Most of them have no idea how to move into their potential because they are so used to playing small. I can totally relate. Staying wrapped in my fear, with low self-esteem, in the throes of addiction or dysfunction was the safest place for me to live before I started my healing journey. Stepping into the daylight of recovery and letting other women nourish and support me gave me the hope and the direction that I needed to plant my life firmly in recovery. I'll be forever grateful for the flowers who came before me.

Risk-taking in recovery creates an entirely different bouquet of life-affirming experiences.

*Although frequently attributed to Anaïs Nin, this quote was actually published by poet Elizabeth Appell in 1979 under the name Lassie Benton.

When We First Meet

If you are a woman in recovery, and I meet you for the first time, I promise to meet with you two things: curiosity and empathy. Regardless of whether we meet via email, in an online meeting, or in person, I'll remain open and interested. I won't presume that I know how you are feeling or what you are bringing to our exchange, or even what you are in recovery from. I will keep in mind that you might bring a history of trauma, that you might be in emotional pain at that moment, or that you might have experience with anxiety or depression. I'll stay open to the possibility that you aren't feeling proud of the first exchanges you've had with other women in recovery, that you might carry shame or regret and be worried that I will judge you. I never will. I'll offer you understanding, and I'll invite you to share what is true for you. I'll let you tell me what you need, and I'll do what I can to point in any direction that might help you get it. This is how recovery works.

I make no assumptions about who you are or what you need, but I'm eager to learn about both things.

• APRIL 26 •

Emotions as Information

I remember being confused by a therapist a few years back when she asked me to pay attention to my emotions to see what they were telling me. I'd had an earlier therapist urge me to feel my darned emotions instead of burying them, and it felt like a step backward to have to start analyzing them. That isn't what she meant. She wasn't asking me to judge or overthink my emotions but rather to view them as clues or indicators to guide how I respond to things. For example, if I feel hurt or angry or even guilty, that's a clue that something isn't right, and I can adjust how I am thinking about or responding to a situation (or both). If I'm feeling joy and excitement, I can see that as an indicator that I need more of whatever it is that brings joy into my life. Emotions don't give us answers. We still need to use our cognitive skills to figure out what our emotions mean, but that is easier to do when we register our feelings and feel them fully.

The more we feel our feelings,
the more comfortable we become
with letting them guide us.

• APRIL 27 •

On Mother Loss

I wasn't always close to my mother, but thanks to my recovery, I had the privilege of closely bonding with her toward the end of her life. Even though she died more than twenty years ago, I still feel the loss each day. The intense pain of the loss fades, but still, I know I'll never be the same. I know for others it's not the loss of the actual relationship that hurts but the loss of the potential; it's the loss of never having been close.

Relationships between mothers and daughters are so complicated. Mothers and daughters are women who lead complex lives that intertwine in both nature and nurture—what we inherit and what we teach. When recovery is part of the relationship, another layer of meaning is added to everything around and between us. These relationships matter.

Before my mother died, she said to me, "You will never get over losing me, but you will get through it." And you know what? My mom was right.

Loss is felt in many ways between
mothers and daughters. It's good to feel,
though it may break our hearts.

On Tears and Prayer

When I was a little Catholic kid, I knew to pray when I really wanted something, especially toys. The clearest praying memory I have had nothing to do with toys. The picture imprinted on my mind is me sitting in the back seat of our car, my mom in the front passenger seat with tears rolling down her face. I was nine years old, and it was the first time I had ever seen her cry. We had just left the hospital after a visit with her father, who was dying. My prayer that day was that my grandfather would live. Not because I loved him, because he wasn't very lovable, but because I couldn't bear to see my mother hurting. Desperate for her to stop crying, I promised god that if "Daddy Tom" lived, I would become a nun.

My grandfather lived. My mom stopped crying. I didn't keep my promise to become a nun, but my belief that prayers might work began that day. To this day, I spend my most fervent prayers on asking my higher power to relieve the pain of people I love. It still works, at times.

Tears and prayers are powerful on their own,
but even more powerful in combination.

• APRIL 29 •

We Recover in Our Own Way

The idea of individualized recovery was nowhere to be found when I completed substance use treatment in the late 1980s. Back then, nobody suggested that addicted women like me should read books, listen to podcasts, join online communities, diffuse essential oils, do hypnotherapy or plant medicine, or embrace running or yoga to heal. There was no recovery management or aftercare plan for me when I left treatment, and nobody even suggested that I should continue to seek professional support. I was advised to find and attend a Twelve Step recovery program. Period.

I am so fortunate that Twelve Step recovery worked for me and that I was privileged enough to be able to access a community of people where I lived who welcomed me, nurtured me, and put up with me. I was a single mom on welfare and had no financial resources for additional treatment or therapy in that moment. Twelve Step recovery helped save my life. I'm so glad it still exists and is still saving literally millions of women's lives. But it isn't for everybody, and the recovery world needs to be okay with that. Period.

We can't demand that everyone recover the same way; that's the opposite of a person-centered approach.

• APRIL 30 •

Into the Fire

I haven't felt prepared for most of the major stages of my life, but I've jumped in with both feet for most of them. Becoming addicted to substances was basically trial by fire; nothing has tested me like the challenges I experienced in those years. I dove into motherhood unexpectedly and unprepared (I did not have either of my two children on purpose), but somehow, I instinctively figured out how to mother. When I entered recovery, I definitely felt like I was out of my league, but over a short period of time I found other women who had learned to tend to their own fires (internal and external) and who were willing to guide and support me. The only area in my life that I feel I am heading into fully intentionally is aging. I have spent a lot of time pondering this, and I don't want to "wing" getting old. I want to be purposeful, not because I need to do it right but because I think my third act must surely be my most important. It's where I get to practice everything that I have learned to date, to simplify things on one hand and maybe go deeper on a few others. I'm ready to jump into the fire of my final chapter. Hopefully with a little bit of grace.

All of my life has been a gift, but I'm excited about the gifts that must surely come with wisdom and experience.

MAY

Cultivating Optimism

One of the mindsets that I really had to work on changing in early recovery was my tendency toward pessimism. I was a bit of a doom-and-gloom type at the end of my active addiction, in large part because life was difficult and sometimes dark. I was a single mother without means, and I was starting a brand-new life that petrified me. I think I focused on what wasn't working to protect myself from further disappointment. I remember a therapist calling me out on my negative expectations and encouraging me to practice finding the good in every situation presented to me. She made me keep a journal and report back to her. I like to think of that exercise as my first gratitude practice. In any case, it blew my mind, and I learned quickly of the benefit of being hopeful and eventually even confident that things could work out. Changing my mindset didn't change my circumstances, but it sure helped me navigate them. I love what psychologist Lucy MacDonald, author of *You Can Be an Optimist*, says about optimism: although optimism can't solve all of our life problems, "it can sometimes make the difference between coping and collapsing."

We can't know if things will turn out well or badly, but let's always hope for the best.

• MAY 2 •

Choose Your Circle

In some recovery communities, there is a saying that goes something like "Stick with the winners." On one level, I get it—it's intended to guide people seeking recovery to hang out with people who are already "succeeding" in their recovery. However, I don't like the implication that there are winners and losers in recovery. Recovery isn't about judging other people's recovery. Anyone seeking or attempting recovery is worthy of respect and support, regardless of what they achieve (or don't) through their efforts.

I prefer to focus on the importance of surrounding ourselves with people who have positive energy. Positive energy is supportive, uplifting, inspiring, and contagious. Creating or joining a circle of woman-identifying individuals whose energy is positive doesn't mean those individuals are perfect, consistently happy, or high achievers in all things. Positive energy also includes energy that is warm, forgiving, and compassionate. You will find your circle of women who are all of these things because you are a woman who is all of these things. Your recovery energy will attract your recovery circle.

As we choose our support system,
so too do we choose our energy.

Releasing the Lies

In recovery, I have had to release a lot of lies about myself and my life to make room for the truth to come in. I spent years of dysfunctional living believing that I was bad, wrong, awful, hopeless. Those are the things that I told myself and what I heard from others who benefited from my low self-worth. The messages were strong, and it wasn't easy to release all these harmful untruths. Therapy helped me unpack the lies. Promiscuity in my teens had a logical explanation: I was merely looking for affection in all the wrong places. Dropping out of university after one year was a trauma response, not a failure of intellect. Dealing drugs was unsafe and illegal, but it was a survival technique. Abortion was another survival response, something that I didn't choose lightly. Being beaten in a relationship was never, ever something that I deserved. I give my therapists credit for helping me to release the old lies that kept me down, but I'm also proud of myself for keeping new lies from creeping in.

Releasing who I am not—and have never been—
brings peace and opens space for truth.

Estrangement

There's something very unnatural about being estranged from a family member. I hope you haven't experienced it, but from what I know, many of us in recovery have. It's heartbreaking and confusing, and even though it started somewhere and with someone, after a while it may be hard to figure out or remember why or when it all began. I've had a few painful estrangements with family members over the course of my recovery. One lasted for five years and was eventually healed because . . . recovery. Hers and mine. A more recent one looks like it might go on forever. I can't fix it, and at this point the fracture has extended to other family members, which is even harder. When I dig through the pain of it all, I know I still love this person and wish them well way over there on the other side of my life. Sometimes space is the thing we need in order to examine and understand a dynamic and where it broke down, and sometimes space is the thing that grows so big there's no way back from it. Time will tell which of the two this is.

Fractured family relationships are hard
for everyone, but if we are fortunate,
sometimes we recover from them.

• MAY 5 •

Be Who You Are

There is a Dr. Seuss quote that goes like this: "Be who you are and say what you feel because those who mind don't matter and those who matter don't mind." I wish that this sentiment could be embraced by every woman in recovery, all the time, but I also understand there are power differentials that mean not all women can claim this. As a woman in recovery from domestic violence, I was not able to be who I was or say what I felt. Today I can, and I do. I probably gave up years of my life when I combine all the hours that I cared about what other people thought of me before I came into recovery. Today, I want the people whom I care about to think well of me, and I'm pretty sure that most do, but you know what? If they don't, I'm okay with that too. I am not a perfect specimen of a person. I mess up here and there, but the people who love and care about me ride those waves of imperfection with me; they don't judge or reject me. Today, I know with my entire being that I just need to be who I am, wherever I am. I hope that you know that you can be who you are and say what you feel too.

I'm just over here being me,
one day at a time.

• MAY 6 •

Being Too Much

There was a time in my life when other people likely viewed me as being too much. I was generally under the influence of substances, I believe, when people thought that about me. I was probably too loud. I might have been too intense. I am sure I appeared too emotional, despite walking around with my feelings completely numbed.

The irony of me being too much in those days was that every action of too-much-ness really had its genesis in me not feeling like I was enough. Being too much was about compensating for not-enough-ness. If I was too much, loved ones couldn't live without me. If I was too much, friends would see how much I had to offer. If I was too much, coworkers and bosses would understand that they needed me on their team in order to succeed.

Being over the top kept me from feeling too low, and being too much was my way of coming out the other side of not being enough. Recovery changed everything. Today, I *am* too much. Too much happy, too much content, too much love.

We are just the right amount of everything when we heal.

Simple Self-Care

What do you think of when you think about self-care? Does it conjure up ideas of a weekend or week away? An expensive day at the spa? Buying yourself flowers? Chocolates? There's nothing wrong with any of those things, but I'm here to remind you that self-care doesn't have to cost you a cent, and you don't have to develop any sort of formal plan to do it. Sitting in silence is self-care. Bonus points if you do it outside in the sun. (Please don't take your phone with you.) If sitting in silence (inside or outside) is hard for you, that's okay. Try it another time. Stretching is also self-care, and I don't mean the kind where you get out your yoga mat. I mean literally stand up and stretch your arms above your head and then bend your neck forward, backward, and then in a circle. Can you try that now? Or modify it to fit your needs if you are not able to stand—you can stretch as you sit in a chair or in bed. Self-care is breathing deeply. Can you take five deep breaths? Count to three on the inhale and five on the exhale. How does that feel? Look at you. You have just rocked simple self-care.

Practice simple self-care throughout the day.
The benefits will astound you.

• MAY 8 •

Practice Small Acts of Generosity

I learned the importance of donating small amounts of money to individuals struggling with homelessness from my dear old friend Larry. Larry and I had spent a portion of our youth selling and doing drugs together, and we went to the same treatment center within one year of each other. One day, when we were both still very new to recovery, we were driving somewhere in downtown Vancouver, British Columbia, when without warning Larry veered the car over to the side, put it into park, and hopped out. He was back within two minutes, and I immediately asked him what the heck he was up to. He replied that every time he drives downtown, he stops and gifts a person on the street a couple of dollars. He does so, he said, simply because he can, and because it feels good. Up until that point, it hadn't occurred to me that even I, with rather meager resources at the time, was still able to help somebody less fortunate. Larry's generosity impacted me greatly, and I've followed in his footsteps for the past thirty years. I don't jump out of my car, but I do hand money out of my window. Larry was right. It feels awesome.

Sharing is caring. Always.

• MAY 9 •

The Possibility of a Higher Power

I was introduced to the concept and value of having a higher power early in my recovery when I embarked on my Twelve Step journey. I didn't believe in a higher power at the time and thought I could recover without one. But the people around me were annoyingly persistent and goaded me into trying to believe in something—*anything*—outside of myself. In my desperation to stop hurting and to get them to leave me alone, I started to experiment. I was informed that my higher power could be anything, so my first one was a small, shiny black rock. Although it felt like complete hogwash, I prayed over the rock for a period of several days. Then I lost the rock. My second higher power was the "universe," which felt more than a little helpful when I practiced "giving things over." Although my higher power remains ever-evolving, I have figured out that the people in my circle were right: believing that there is a force outside of me that I can turn to is an enormous help in my recovery.

Believing in something outside of myself
can bring me back to myself.

• MAY 10 •

Being "Twired"

My friend Nikole introduced me to the term *twired* (tired + wired) one day, and I realized that I'd been searching for that word my entire life. As a person diagnosed with generalized anxiety disorder, I often find myself in a state of twired-ness. It's that feeling—perhaps you know it—of going through something particularly joyous or maybe even deathly hard, and you are simply unable to regulate, incapable of settling into a calm presence. Everything feels outside of my window of tolerance. At times like this, I'm usually physically exhausted, and my body cries out for rest, but my brain is still on high alert or even overload. There is a fight between my body and my mind, and neither is willing to concede. I haven't found the perfect treatment for being twired yet, but drinking a lot of water, going for a walk, and listening to violin music are a few things that help me regulate. How do you recover from being twired?

Being tired and wired at the same time can be confusing. Tread back toward yourself gently.

That Other F-Word

*Trigger warning for anyone with an eating disorder: examination of the word *fat.*

I could have died once upon a time when I was wasting away on drugs, so it stands to reason that I believe having some fat on my bones is a good thing. Why are so many of us afraid of being or getting fat? I love the quote by Cheryl Strayed, who tells us to stop worrying about whether we're fat. As she says, "Who gives a shit?" I grew up thinking that *fat* was a bad word and that I shouldn't use it. In fact, I don't think I ever heard my mother use it. She did, however, say things like "So-and-so has become an awful size" when I'm pretty sure she meant so-and-so had gotten fat. God bless her, she had a few weird ways about her, my mom. I would hazard a guess that so-and-so would have rather been called "fat" than "an awful size." One of the things that I love about the anti-diet movement is that it encourages us to reclaim the word *fat.* I'm not always able to use it comfortably yet, but I'm trying. I'm a little bit fat these days, and I don't give a shit. Thanks, Cheryl.

As we take back our bodies, we get to reclaim language that was once deemed derogatory or shameful.

• MAY 12 •

Making Room for What Matters

I don't know about you, but my days usually fill up very easily without any effort at all on my part. The hours between waking and sleeping fly by. For years, I just went with the flow, let the days take me where they needed to, let the days roll into nights with me exhausted and feeling a little bit deprived, not having spent time doing the things that I really loved to do. Now, I try to be more intentional with my days.

These days, I try hard to make room for what really matters. I'll be honest: I do not always succeed. I'm a recovering workaholic, which means I have to try a lot harder than your average person not to work. But at least once, maybe twice a day, and sometimes even three, I do seriously attempt to make room for what matters. The things that matter to me change, and regardless of what those things are, making room for them may never come naturally. But I sure do feel better when I make it happen.

Try to make room for what matters to you today.
Always remember: you matter to you.

• MAY 13 •

Finding Presence

In her beautiful book *Present over Perfect: Leaving behind Frantic for a Simpler, More Soulful Way of Living*, Shauna Niequist writes about things that many of us who overwork ourselves into burnout can well relate to. In particular, she writes about living her life as if she were a workhorse, giving away her "best energy" to things that were completely outside of herself. One of her regrets about having lived that way for years was that she had "bruised people" with her "fragmented, anxious presence." I feel that description in the depths of my being. I am a person who tries extremely hard not to have regrets and to forgive myself for not doing better when I didn't know better, but I am certain that I, too, have bruised the people I love when I have expended so much of my energy on external issues, projects, or work. I can't go back and revise or recapture my lack of presence in the lives of my loved ones, but now I work hard every day to show up for them.

I try to be here now, as fully but
imperfectly as I can be.

Celebrating Women Doing Less

Are you amazed when you see what some women in recovery are accomplishing? Are you inspired when you watch them go back to school, start a new business, travel the world, or do incredible things selflessly for humanity? I am amazed and inspired to watch them too, but I also worry that for some of us it might be intimidating to see such frenzied success. I also am cautious about us celebrating productivity over . . . well, nonproductivity.

I get filled up when I see women share about how they are resting. How they are sitting in their yard or at a park and reading a book or just staring into space. How they have just told somebody that they are not going to help with something for the tenth year in a row. I love it when women share that they are taking a staycation and filling it up with nothingness. As someone who tends to do too much, I celebrate anyone who can show me how to do less. It's a skill that we should all learn to perfect. Accomplishing less is a major accomplishment. Don't let anyone tell you differently.

Embrace doing less. You have earned the right.

Having Reservations

Before I got to recovery, I thought reservations were just something you had to have when you wanted to go out to eat. But no. Having reservations about recovery means you aren't completely committed to the idea of staying in recovery. For example, having a reservation about recovery from substance use disorder might look something like "I'm never going to drink again unless my marriage ends." For others, having a reservation in recovery means just not being convinced that your recovery is forever, maybe taking an "I'll see how it goes" approach. When it comes to my recovery from a substance use disorder, I can honestly say I have zero reservations about my recovery; I am committed to it for the rest of my life. Some people would challenge me on that, call me cocky, warn me not to be so confident. They can say what they want. I'm in this for life.

A long time ago, I promised myself I would stay in recovery. Recovery helps me keep my promises to myself.

Don't Knock It If You Haven't Tried It

I understand that Twelve Step programs aren't perfect and that they aren't going to work for everyone. And that's perfectly okay. However, I still recommend that every woman in recovery check out a Twelve Step meeting (related to whatever she is recovering from) at least once. I can still conjure up how it felt when I first found those meetings and was able to sit among women (and men) and share my fears, wounds, and hopes. I found my voice in my Twelve Step program. For that time in my life, following treatment, "the rooms" provided me with a place where I was able to identify and share feelings freely for almost the first time in my life. For the first year or so that I attended meetings, I cried at almost every meeting, and it felt so good to release those tears. Early recovery was hard, but doing hard things with support was something brand new to me, and I'll treasure those times always. It's hard not to be grateful to the thing that helped breathe life back into me. If you've never attended a Twelve Step program, I recommend you try one, even if only to say that you have done so. No commitment required.

Don't let other people's opinions and attitudes keep you from investigating any recovery modality. Only you know what is going to work for you; try everything available to you.

Adding Play to Our Day

Part of reconnecting with our inner child in recovery is learning how to play again. In our She Recovers community, we've tossed around the idea of having a She Recovers summer camp so that we can all come together and learn or relearn how to play, to practice being carefree and joyous. I can picture it now: splashing and swimming in a lake, making crafts, and playing camp games. One day, that camp will be a reality, but for now, we need to find other ways to embrace play. My little grandson is a great teacher in this area. That boy laughs and plays by himself for hours at a time. He plays with cups and a *Paw Patrol* figure for hours in the bathtub, or with a shovel and pail at the beach, mindfully filling the pail with sand, dumping it out, and starting again. He is partial to trucks these days, but stacking books one upon the other is also a favorite pastime. It occurs to me as I write this that I am often more an observer than a participant in this little guy's play. I'm going to change that.

Playing nourishes our souls,
no matter our age.

• MAY 18 •

Dance

Our She Recovers community will be forever grateful to our dearest friend Payton for creating a beautiful dance / guided movement that can be offered at in-person events or online. Sharing space as we move our bodies to fabulous music promotes self-discovery, body positivity, freedom, joy, and empowerment. And it's fun! For those of us who used to dance without reservation while under the influence, it can take a minute to feel comfortable dancing substance-free. But Payton and the other dance facilitators invite us to explore five pillars of this unique dance practice. *Willingness* to explore our own unique movement practice. *Curiosity* over criticism as we allow movement to bring more self-acceptance and self-love to our recovery. *Acceptance* of our bodies and movement abilities just as they are, and *joy* and *freedom* to express our own authentic self. This dance practice is playful, inspiring, and judgment-free. I highly recommend it.

Recovery entails exploring the practice of listening to and learning how we can comfortably move our bodies. We might as well do it to music!

Strengths over Defects

When I first got into recovery, the program that I belonged to—the one that saved my life—emphasized the importance of working on my character defects. That concept resonated for me because, at the time, I felt like I was just one big, walking defect. It felt natural for me to ask questions and try to fix those things that were wrong about me, to dig into all the things that I did or didn't do that created problems for me. Don't get me wrong; I needed to become aware of thoughts, habits, and behaviors that didn't serve me or hurt me or others. That remains true today. I will always have something to work on. But as I've grown in recovery, what I have found to be helpful is that focusing on my strengths and the things that I am doing well yields much better outcomes than focusing on where I fall short.

Have you experienced something similar in your journey? Has it seemed easier to see the negatives instead of the positives? That's also part of our growth. Our self-talk moves from negative to positive as we grow and learn to trust ourselves more.

What receives attention grows.
I choose to focus on my strengths.

Can We Love Someone Too Much?

One of the most heartbreaking things that I have experienced in my recovery is watching people love family members or other loved ones who are experiencing a deadly addiction. I see them try everything and give everything to try to help their addicted person recover. Sometimes it works, but other times nothing works, and they end up deeply unwell themselves. It becomes an exhausting, constant, and difficult negotiation between loving and supporting the person and taking care of themselves. It's hard—and sometimes impossible—to do both well.

My friend Alicia Cook is a writer, speaker, and activist who tirelessly spreads awareness about how drug addiction impacts entire families. In her powerful poem "A Prayer for the Codependent," she reminds us that we can love the people in our lives who are struggling the mightiest, but there are times when loving them too much can in fact harm them. As Alicia poignantly writes, "I will stand firm in your corner when no one else is left, but I will not be the one who loves you to death."

Our codependency tells us that we can love
a person to wellness, but that is a lie.

• MAY 21 •

On Therapy

I've come to know that therapy is more about revisiting our core issues than resolving them. When I hit the wall with workaholism in 2011, I embarked on a two-year therapy journey to figure out how I had ended up so addicted to work that I had decimated my mental, physical, and spiritual health and nearly destroyed my marriage and family life. After just a couple of sessions, my therapist posed the question "Why do you think that your value as a person is based on how much you work or produce?" I didn't have an answer until after I'd spent two years and a fair bit of money working with that therapist.

Fast-forward to the present: imagine my surprise when I recently read an old journal entry of mine from 1991 and discovered that, a full twenty years before that therapist, I had written about something that she had helped me figure out, which was that I found my self-worth "only in what I do, and not who I am." Remarkable that I hadn't made much progress over twenty years. But I'm doing better now and have learned that sometimes we don't see what we need to understand until we're ready to understand it.

Therapy is a little bit of déjà vu
and a lot of hard work.

• MAY 22 •

Never Question the Decision

My friend Holly Whitaker, author of *Quit Like a Woman: The Radical Choice to Not Drink in a Culture Obsessed with Alcohol,* has helped make the saying "Never question the decision" popular in the recovery community. She has written and spoken about it as meaning "Never question the decision to get sober or to recover—once you have made that decision, just go with it." I get where she is coming from, and I think she's brilliant. The thing about recovery, especially if it's recovery from substance issues, is you can spend an awful lot of time in your head asking yourself, *Was it really that bad? Can I really never do that again? What if I just did this or what if I just did that? What if I only had one?* It's a lot easier to leave those thoughts alone, to just remind yourself you've made the decision that you aren't going to drink, smoke pot, gamble, overwork, or call up that person who doesn't deserve you. Treat your decision as a given, don't give it space or energy, shut down those questioning thoughts as they arise. Keep your commitment to yourself.

There was a reason you made the decision in the first place. Trust it.

Many Roads

Charlotte Kasl's 1992 book *Many Roads, One Journey: Moving Beyond the 12 Steps* was a rich rethinking of how women could be supported to recover from addiction and/or codependency. An addiction specialist and psychotherapist, Kasl focused on holistic and diverse approaches to recovery. Her analysis had gender as its starting point, but she also incorporated class, race, sexual orientation, and culture into her framework. Especially groundbreaking for the time, Kasl's book emphasized the importance of tending to the body in recovery with a focus on nutrition and movement.

Kasl's book is timeless, and so are her ideas. If you haven't read the book or been introduced to Kasl's 16 Steps for Discovery and Empowerment, I suggest you find time to investigate both. The modern women's recovery movement has its roots in the inspired work of the women who have recovered before us. How fortunate are we?

We stand on the shoulders of
other women in recovery.

Right Now

Time for a check-in. What do you need to do for yourself right now, today? Do you have a full day planned? Can you build in something you can do just for yourself? Something nurturing or stress-reducing if you are feeling overwhelmed or something inspiring or exciting if you are feeling bored? Do you need to take a walk or a nap? Have a snack? The likelihood that anybody else is going to figure out what you need and then make sure you get it is, I'm sorry to say, very slim. But I bet if you close your eyes and ask yourself the question "What do I need today?" that something will come to you. It can't hurt to try.

Let your intuition tell you what you need
and your sense of worthiness ensure
that you get it.

• MAY 25 •

The Irony of My Addiction

Once upon a time, I was a confused teenager deathly afraid of even experimenting with the very substances that would come to rule my life. Desperate to fit in somewhere, to be accepted, or perhaps just to be noticed, when the other fifteen-year-olds that I hung out with started to drink at parties, I pretended to drink and then feigned being drunk. The first time I was offered a tab of acid, I faked swallowing it and then acted as if I, too, were seeing purple dinosaurs dance across the walls. Pretending to smoke pot the first few times was a little more difficult, but I didn't inhale. My instincts were right; I had much to fear from drugs and alcohol. Like many women, I ignored my instincts and listened to my own shadows. Predictably, things worked out for the worse. The great irony, of course, was that toward the end of my first spiral of addiction, much of my energy went into pretending that I was not under the influence of substances. I'm so grateful not to have to pretend in either direction anymore when it comes to substances.

Trust your true instincts;
they seldom steer you wrong.

• MAY 26 •

Nurturing Healthy Relationships

I was recently introduced to the idea of relational self-care, and I quite like it. I've done a lot of work to develop and sustain meaningful, healthy relationships since I've been in recovery, but I hadn't ever really thought of relationships as a self-care domain. It works, though. It suggests a certain element of intention in how we approach relationships and work to enhance interpersonal connections, but it also suggests a lovely way of thinking about how relationships nurture us (self-care). Practicing relational self-care includes prioritizing relationships with our spouses, partners, children, and other important family members and friends. It's about seeking and accepting emotional support, and, in reciprocity, providing practical and emotional support to others. I think it also entails letting go of unhealthy relationships (as hard as that can be) and maybe putting effort into establishing, sustaining, or deepening important friendships with like-hearted and like-minded people. Caring for our relationships and caring about how we are in relationships is good self-care. How would you rate your ability to practice relational self-care these days?

Relationships can nurture and sustain us
if we practice relational self-care.

Caring for Our Spiritual Selves

When I first got into recovery, I somehow picked up the idea that the goal of recovery was to become super spiritual. Problem was, I didn't really know what that meant. I suspected that it had something to do with becoming a perfect human being who was always compassionate and incredibly wise. I no longer aspire to any such state of spiritual perfection. But I do subscribe to the notion that caring for our spiritual selves is one of the most nurturing things that we can do for ourselves. Perhaps your spiritual self-care is rooted in faith or religious affiliation; perhaps it's a secular pursuit. Maybe you participate in ceremonial practices and sacred customs that are a part of your culture. There's no wrong way to do spiritual self-care. Spiritual practice for me is about creating space to reflect on my inner needs and my role or place within the world or universe. It's about practicing and expressing gratitude. It often involves meditation. It's about writing. Walking in nature. Moon gazing. How do you practice spiritual self-care?

Those things that nurture your spirit?
Do them often.

Becoming Our Own Best Friend

In a certain sense, recovery from any of the things that we recover from is about learning how to become our own best friend. Making friends with ourselves is not an easy concept for us to grasp initially, but we figure it out eventually. We befriend ourselves by stopping the behaviors that are causing us harm, then doing the work that we need to do to heal our traumas and, over time, release our past. We befriend ourselves by treating ourselves kindly and with appreciation—the same ways that we treat other friends in our life. After years of being our own worst enemy, becoming our own best friend is a relief and an opportunity. It opens the door to self-care, self-compassion, and, over time, self-love. Becoming our own best friend is an important milestone in our healing. After all, we can never have too many friends, right?

Are you your own best friend? If not, can you practice treating yourself as you would treat a dear friend?

An Honor and an Obligation

This world is waiting for all of us to show up and be a part of a global healing project. We need to heal our earth, our politics, our communities, our families, and ourselves. But not in that order. At this moment in history, the imperative is for all of us as individual, diverse, and empowered women to be intentional about defining our own recovery, curating our own healing patchwork pieces, reaching our self-actualization, and then sharing what works with other women. What an honor it is to be able to show up and make a difference. But we can only heal the collective if we heal our own hearts first.

We may not think that our unique contributions will have an impact. We tell ourselves that there is too much wrong with the world to make a dent. That's not true. There is a lot right with the world, and any single thing we do to make it better will touch someone or affect something. We just need to remember and repeat often that when women heal, families heal, and communities heal too. How are you showing up to do that?

The world is waiting for each of us to start or continue our healing journey.

Never Too Old

When I first got into recovery for substance use issues, I was twenty-seven years old. I knew that I needed to change my life, but there was a part of me that thought it was too late. It wasn't, because the truth is that it is never too late to stop killing ourselves with poisonous substances. Several years later, I had an opportunity to go back to university to finish a degree that I had abandoned in my addiction. I thought I was too old. I wasn't. I stayed in university for thirteen years, and when I finished my final degree at forty-five, I felt that I was running out of time to establish myself in a career. That wasn't true either. After fifteen years of writing professionally, I knew for sure I was too old to start writing books. Apparently, that was also untrue. Here's the thing. Recovery opens us up to a multitude of opportunities regardless of how old we are. That thing that you think you are too old to tackle? I'm guessing you aren't too old at all. What is that thing? Can you write about it? Can you tell somebody about it? Can you do one small thing to move toward it?

Carpe diem (seize the day). It's only too late after you have taken your last breath.

• MAY 31 •

Don't Force Things That Don't Fit

You know how sometimes we work so hard to make something happen or fit, and it just isn't working? How do we know when it's time to stop forcing things? Do we keep trying to jam ourselves into that job where we feel devalued or the relationship where we can't really be ourselves? Do we even want those things that we know can only be ours if we force them to be? If we trust our gut, we know when the level of energy we are expending is both too much and still not enough to get to the outcome that we think we want. I can never remember if that saying (you know the one) is about trying to fit a square peg into a round hole or a round peg into a square hole, but either way, it's never going to happen, and we cannot will it to. I've had to step away from a lot of things in my recovery after wearing myself out trying to force them to happen. It was exhausting. I try not to do that anymore.

There are always clues about what is meant for us and what is not. Tap into your knowing and act accordingly.

JUNE

Dear Eight-Year-Old Me

Hey, little me. I wish I could reach back in time and give you a hug. I know that you feel invisible in your family, and I'm sorry that you are growing up without having your emotional needs met. You deserve to have every one of your needs met. I want you to know that your parents are doing their best, but it's okay to admit that their best isn't good enough here.

I wish that you could feel their love, and one day you will come to know that it was always there. For now, they are too preoccupied with grown-up issues, and their own childhood wounds get in the way of them expressing or responding to feelings. I see you trying so hard to get their attention, and I feel your hurt when they fail to give it. I'm glad that you get noticed at school, that your teacher recognizes how bright you are and that you get to feel her caring and approval. Keep on with your love of reading and writing. One day your words may help someone else.

Just keep on going, little one.
The best is yet to come.

Not Everything Happens for a Reason

There was a time in my life, and in my recovery, when I used to spout the platitude that "everything happens for a reason." Thinking that was true somehow gave me comfort when I didn't get my way on something, but I also pulled out the phrase to comfort others when bad things happened to them. I no longer believe or say that when bad things happen, and please accept my apology now if I ever said that to you in the past. I think of my friend Deanna who lost her beloved daughter Morgan and unborn grandson Isaiah to an accidental overdose, and I can't think of a single reason in this universe why that happened. Why do we think it's important to reason away tragedies and losses that we can't personally comprehend? Can we relate to how traumatic it might be for a grieving mother or person to hear that their loss is somehow part of a wider cosmic plan? Some things happen for a reason, but not everything. Maybe that's just as comforting to know.

We may find a way to go on after loss,
but we don't need to reason away the loss.

• JUNE 3 •

Being of Service

I learned the importance of being of service in my Twelve Step program. But actually, I had been introduced to the concept long before. When I was a Brownie, the motto for Brownies was "Lend a hand." I grew up hearing in church about being a Good Samaritan, about doing good deeds. Those messages stuck with me, even when I wasn't able to practice them.

Being of service in recovery can mean a lot of different things. Being of service is always about contributing to something bigger than ourselves. It can be volunteering; it might be caregiving or helping the people we love. We can be of service with our ideas, we can share our thoughts, we can share words, we can share actions. We can be of service at home but also outside our home. Being of service is about getting outside of ourselves.

Being of service in recovery also requires that we know our limits, that we don't give so much of ourselves away that we are depleted. We aren't any good to others if we don't take care of ourselves.

I will look for opportunities
to be of service today.

• JUNE 4 •

Strolling over Scrolling

I have a problem with scrolling. I don't know about you, but I practice obsessive use of scrolling with my iPhone. It is possible to become addicted to technology. What are we doing when we're scrolling? Sure, there is a good side to social networking, especially when we connect with others in recovery or find inspiration or ideas that help us. But the mindless scrolling? The doom scrolling? When we use it as a replacement for reality? We're numbing. Social media is a time suck.

It's time to get honest about our scrolling. What if we disrupt our scrolling and move? Movement is medicine. What would it feel like for you to put down your phone, leave it at home or in your office, and walk around the block? Are you willing to try that? Can you do it right now? There is a wonderful quote by Karen Ann Kennedy: "Unplug to unwind; tune out to tune in; and disconnect to connect." What if we tried that? Get outside. The sky is the best light.

Like everything that is addictive,
scrolling serves a purpose . . .
until it doesn't.

The Gifts of Rest

At its core, resting is about *being* and not *doing*. It's about slowing down, breathing, setting devices aside, pausing and being still, being quiet. We often equate resting with sleeping, and getting enough sleep at night or taking a nap can be part of resting, but they aren't the whole enchilada.

Some people think that resting is an unproductive waste of time, but the opposite is true. Rest is a gift you give yourself, full stop. But if productivity is important to you, you should know that you will always be more productive on the other side of rest. You are better off to rest before you get tired. When we're tired, we're more susceptible to all sorts of things, like drawing on coping mechanisms that don't serve us. When we're tired, we pull from adrenaline for energy. Do you know what that means? We make things exciting—we manufacture excitement—so we can pull some energy from it. How about we manufacture energy by resting?

Can you schedule rest breaks throughout your day so that you can relax, refresh, or recover? Treat time as your friend. Lose any guilt you have about resting.

Rest is a crucial part of recovery.

• JUNE 6 •

Name It to Claim It

Over the past many years, I've read and heard a lot of talk about manifesting. People talk or write about manifesting what they want in their lives, manifesting relationships, and manifesting dreams. I know that this idea is empowering for many people, and if that's the case for you, I respect that. I have indeed seen people I love manifest some cool things. However, the word has gotten to be a little bit annoying for me, perhaps because it's been so overused. I support the underlying concept, but I need to give it my own twist. Whereas manifesting seems to be more about thinking things into existence, saying out loud what we really want feels more powerful to me. I say things out loud to myself, and I'm inspired; I say things out loud to you and the universe, and the energy in the air changes. It's like talking about recovery. I share messages about recovery out loud, and it furthers my ownership of recovery. I name it to claim it. What are you naming today in hopes of claiming it? Can you say it out loud?

Naming what I want and how I want it
is just a start, but it's a powerful start.

• JUNE 7 •

In My Footsteps and Beyond

I have worked so hard to change my family's story and succeeded in many ways. Still, my heart shattered into a million pieces when I saw my youngest daughter, Taryn, repeat during her adolescence patterns of addiction that I'd hoped and prayed would end with me. But our children have their own stories and lives to live. I don't take for granted that Taryn survived her addiction, and I am grateful every day for her recovery. As the co-founder of our She Recovers movement, Taryn provides a younger—dare I admit *edgier*—road map for wellness. It's been one of my greatest honors to watch my daughter design her own pathways and patchwork of recovery, heal herself, and lead others back to themselves too. I have learned a lot from this unique child of mine, this beautiful, bright, compassionate, and driven person who is both like me and the total opposite of me. I watch in awe and wonder what she will do next.

Of my body and of my heart, my youngest daughter is one of my greatest teachers in recovery.

• JUNE 8 •

Owning Who We Are

We learn how to tell the truth in recovery. That can mean figuring out how to tell really big truths about ourselves, which includes naming and owning who we are. Over the years, I have supported friends in recovery coming out (literally) and naming some really big truths about their sexuality and identity. It's a beautiful thing to witness. I've been there for friends who faced and owned some hard truths about long-term relationships as well as changed their preferences for what they want to do for work. Knowing what we want and what we like invites change, and in recovery we can accept those invitations. I have had a few major awakenings about preferences over the past few decades, but it's the little things I speak up about these days that feed my sense of self. Not too long ago, I admitted to my partner that I don't like pancakes, although I had eaten them most weekends for thirty years because he and our kids loved them. I longed for tradition, and pancakes felt like tradition. I'm getting to an age now where I just don't have time to pretend to like things anymore. So pancakes are out. Oddly enough, waffles are still in.

Recovery helps us get at our likes and dislikes and shows us how to express them more clearly.

• JUNE 9 •

Storytelling as a Recovery Pathway

My friend Meghann Perry is passionate about promoting the *practice* of storytelling in the recovery community as a powerful tool for connection, personal transformation, and social justice. Storytelling is both a potent practice and an art form, and Meghann's work is dedicated to promoting storytelling as another "beautiful thread in our universal tapestry of recovery and community." We cannot disagree with that. Sharing our stories with other people in recovery, and listening to theirs, is an art form with deep therapeutic value.

Meghann reminds us that most of us carry a "personal mythology" into recovery with us—a core belief system about ourselves that is often accurate. She facilitates powerful storytelling events and workshops that lead individuals to question what is true and what is not in the myths that have come to rule how we feel about ourselves and how we act in relation to those myths. Questioning those stories and myths must be a key focus at some time in our recovery. Doing this work in community is powerful, not only for us personally, but for the recovery community and the world beyond it. What myths have you told yourself? Have you shared them with others?

We can heal our lives and our communities,
one story at a time.

Designing Prayer Rituals

I am not one of them, but I honor people who are nurtured by deep religious faith. If that is you, I'm glad for you. If you have been traumatized by religion, I'm so very sorry. I am a lapsed Catholic with lingering emotional attachment to some of what my late Irish Catholic grandmother taught me about praying. My prayer rituals honor my love for her but are guided by my own preferences. Sometimes I use a rosary in my "counting my blessings" practice; other times I use a mala (a meditation garland). I pray to the Virgin Mary as often as I pray to my dead mother. I also pray or make devout petitions to the sunrise, the clouds in the sky, or the trees in my backyard. I have been known to write my prayers on a piece of paper and throw them in a fire, surrounded by women in recovery who are doing the same. Some might not consider what I do as true prayer; others might call it "prayer lite." It only matters that it works for me.

How we pray can be as individualized
as who or what we pray to.

• JUNE 11 •

The Discomfort of Self-Discovery

There are two things that I don't love about self-discovery. The first is that it is hard work, and the second is that it is never-ending. I've been asking myself "Who am I?" since the day I got into recovery—probably before, but the time before recovery is rather a blur. The work of self-discovery, as I've figured out, is about examining my life, figuring out what is working well, and doing more of that, then identifying what I am missing in life and figuring out how to incorporate it. The uncomfortable part for me is more about the process than the results of the examination. I have a hard time discovering more of myself by myself. When I head into a new period of self-discovery (often with a therapist), I head in nervously because I know that I am going to find out some things about myself that will make me uncomfortable and will require me to do more work. And sometimes I just don't want to do the work. I wish that the answer to "Who am I?" was consistent, but life is more interesting than that.

Self-discovery doesn't happen accidentally;
it takes effort. And it's worth it.

• JUNE 12 •

The Gift of Solitude

I could never be alone in the years when I was in active addiction or dysfunction, and I never wanted to be. I thought that wanting time alone was somehow anti-social. Nothing feels further from the truth for me today. As I've grown in my recovery, it's become apparent to me that one of my absolute favorite things to do is spend several days in a row in complete solitude. The pandemic cemented how true this was for me, and the uncertainty surrounding the pandemic reminded me how important it is to make time for what we love and need. Taking some time in solitude is a gift that we give ourselves; it's not as likely that others in our life will gift it to us. We can use the time to rest, to refuel, to create, or to be completely unproductive. The gift is in the freedom of doing solely what we want or need. I know it's not easy for most to carve out days of solitude, but if you can, try to carve out at least an hour in solitude here and there. You will thank yourself.

One of the greatest gifts of recovery is learning to love being with ourselves.

• JUNE 13 •

Making a "To-Undo" List

For years I've preached the value of having a "not-to-do" list if you are a person who does too much. It requires taking a second look at your daily to-do list and taking things off it to lighten your day. It works! Recently I came across another idea for a list that I think is worth talking about. This one is not focused so much on our daily lives as it is on our broader experience. It's called the "to-undo" list, and I found it on an Instagram account called *@crazyheadcomics,* created by a mental health advocate in Sweden. The to-undo list might be longer and harder to address than any to-do or not-to-do list, so I think it's a powerful concept. The things that *@crazyheadcomics* recommends putting on our to-undo list include generational trauma, settling for things that aren't for us, always waiting for the perfect time, doubting our worth, our fear of failure, and treating our anxious thoughts as facts. Now there's an undo list that we can all get behind. Right?

Undoing those things that no longer
serve us takes time, but it's doable.

• JUNE 14 •

Navigating Uncertainty

Sometimes life needs to be lived minute by minute, second by second. Sometimes things are uncertain, and uncertainty is one of my triggers. I can't tolerate it. Instead, I trend toward excessive worry. The ambiguity feels intolerable. It's hard to take up space in the waiting. My anxiety kicks in when things are unknown, and I fall into old behaviors like overworking to try to regulate. It's not a helpful approach.

When I'm feeling unmoored in uncertainty, I need to ask myself, *Am I craving clarity, or do I crave control?* There's so much we cannot know. So much we'll never know. Knowing this makes it easier to come to the next stage of coping with uncertainty: acceptance. I accept that I can't control everything. I can't always have clarity. I can't always have certainty. I can accept all of this because I trust myself. I will make good decisions in my recovery, whatever the circumstances. Living through a pandemic was a good exercise in navigating uncertainty for all of us. But navigating uncertainty is never easy for a control freak.

Today, I try to flow with uncertainty
rather than try to outsmart it.

• JUNE 15 •

Coming to Believe

I read Shakti Gawain's book *Creative Visualization* very soon after it came out in 1978. Although I was deep in my addiction to drugs and chaos at the time, a part of me —which I understand now to be the truest part of me— connected to Gawain's teaching that we can use affirmations and mental imagery to guide us toward positive change. A decade or so later, I returned to the practice of creative visualization as part of my early recovery journey. I came to believe, and still do, that painting a picture of something in my head, imagining it, and pretending it is real helps give me the confidence to move firmly in its direction. Just thinking or visualizing doesn't make it happen, but coming to believe that it can be mine, whatever it is, supports and motivates me to move forward and into action. That's how visualization works for me. Does visualization work for you? Try to visualize one of your goals right now.

Visualizing something helps me believe that
it can be mine and gives me the impetus
I need to move toward it.

• JUNE 16 •

Letting Go with Trust

Learning how to let go has been a big part of my recovery. Letting go of expectations, letting go of what others think about me, letting go of what others are doing or not doing, letting go of the results of my work once I put it out into the world—the list goes on. For someone who spent years tightly hanging on to control wherever I could, letting go did not come easily or naturally. Fortunately, early in recovery, I hung out with people who were practicing this thing called the Third Step, which is, quite simply, letting go of control or letting go of trying to control an outcome. The language that a lot of people used then, as now, is "Let go and let god," but I know that isn't going to work for everyone. It didn't work for me when I first heard it. Today, letting go means allowing everyone to be themselves and be responsible for their own lives and decisions. It can also mean taking a leap to do something when I'm deathly afraid to do it.

I can let go, turn things over, and trust that even if things fail or I fall, something or someone will be there to catch me.

• JUNE 17 •

Our Changing Stories

Our stories change over time. As we grow older and wiser, we gain a better understanding of who we are and what happened to us, and we get to revisit our story—the one we tell ourselves and the one we share with others. Brené Brown says, "Owning our story can be hard, but not nearly as difficult as spending our lives running from it." I stopped running from my story when I got into recovery. I haven't loved all the new pieces of my story that have been revealed to me since, whether those pieces came to me from someone else's telling or emerged through some therapist's skillful guidance. I am inclined to leave various details out when I share my story, not because those details have power over me or cause me shame but because some parts of my story are deeply entwined with other people's stories, and it's not my place to write or talk about what happened for them. I own my story and I'm proud of it. I'm curious to see how my story ends.

This is my story, and I'm sticking to it.
What's yours? Are you owning it?

Check on Your Humans

I have accumulated a heck of a lot of humans over the decades of my recovery. My inner circle is quite large, and there are circles around that inner circle filled with even more like-minded, like-hearted women whom I am grateful to call friends. I don't see most of my recovery friends in person all that often, but when I do, it's amazing. Occasionally, a woman's name or face will pop into my head, and I'll realize that I haven't heard from her in months or years. It takes absolutely nothing for me to send her a quick text (if I have her phone number) or a message on a social media platform. Usually, I'll hear back that it was nice to be thought of and that all is good. But sometimes I get a response that goes something like this: "I can't believe you are messaging me right now. I'm not doing well. How did you know?" Of course, I didn't know, but I'm always grateful for whatever energy in the universe led me to reach out to her. When was the last time you reached out to one of your humans? Can you do it today?

It's nice to be thought of, and it's just as nice to be the one doing the thinking.

• JUNE 19 •

Health Scares Are Scary, Yet Helpful

Recovering from cancer was one of the most amazing things that I ever got to do in my life. That said, I would prefer not to have to do it again. Even several decades later, I still occasionally get seized with fear that my cancer is back. Every strange symptom or blood test result has the power to unleash my deepest fears, but I've figured out a few tricks for dealing with health scares. First, I remind myself that none of the scares I've had since I was treated for cancer in 2005 have turned out to be cancer. The second thing I do, and just as important (hear me out, this might sound weird), is that I walk myself through what would happen if the cancer scare turned into real cancer. How would I feel about where I'm at in my life and how I am using my time here on earth? I'm telling you, it gives me pause and reminds me that old age is not promised to us. So, as scary as it is to think my cancer may be back, it reminds me to make the most of the life that I was spared from losing so many years ago.

Making the years matter matters to me,
but I have to take them one day at a time.

• JUNE 20 •

Active Listening

My partner tells me that I'm a terrible listener in our relationship. I think he's probably right. I can tell you how you *should* listen, but I admit I don't always practice these things. Active listening is neutral and nonjudgmental; it's patient. We don't notice our own silence because we are giving verbal and nonverbal feedback through smiling and eye contact (although it's important to point out that making eye contact is seen as disrespectful in some cultures). Active listening is about asking questions and asking for clarification; it's about summarizing. It's also important that you listen with all your senses so you can listen for what is *not* being said too.

Actively listening to *others* is just one type of active listening. It's every bit as important that we listen actively to *ourselves.* In recovery, we can hear our inner voice and encourage it to speak loudly. We can smile at ourselves. We can nod and be nonjudgmental. We can ask ourselves questions. We're sure to have some kickass answers.

Active listening supports healthier interactions with others as well as with ourselves.

• JUNE 21 •

Summer

I have a nostalgic attachment to summer because I remember it as being such a joyful time in my childhood. Despite the family dysfunction, mosquito bites, sunburns, and unbearable humidity of the East Coast town where I was raised, summers were fun. We had a big pool, and our backyard was filled with cousins, Kool-Aid, and hot dogs every weekend from June through September. Those were some of the happiest weekends of my young life. I live clear across the country these days, and I still love summer. Recovery has taught me to appreciate and be present for the best that season has to offer. I love the smell of cut grass, even though I'm allergic to it. I love the sunshine that lasts long into the night. I love that I can get to the beach in ten minutes. I love Saturday drives out into the country, the farm stands, the corn, and all the fresh fruit and vegetables. I love hanging out at home with friends, family, and especially my grandkids. The backyard menu no longer includes Kool-Aid, and the pool is just a kiddie pool, but I know those kids are making memories that will last their lifetime too.

Every season of the year, and of our lives,
has its own highlights.

Achievement Attachment

I haven't always been an overachiever, but I think I've always been achievement focused. I've achieved some big things. My drive to achieve has led to some remarkable successes personally, career-wise and education-wise. But if I'm honest, it's also driven me to neglect relationships, family, love, leisure, and health. Being achievement-attached is like being success-driven. An unhealthy focus on winning gets nobody anywhere and requires intense energy. We get addicted to accumulating achievements—academic, professional, creative. Really, it's just another term for workaholism. And like anything we do too much of that comes with a side of dopamine, achieving feels fantastic, but coming down is hard.

But I didn't become this way in a vacuum. It took self-reflection to see what achievement actually got me: love and attention. I earned attention only when I achieved. I became addicted to the recognition of the things I do. Once I saw the connection, I could work on detaching from achievement. Now, I don't need to be recognized for what I do today. My greatest achievement is self-love.

What do I need when I seek achievement?
Is a win a win, or is it more than that?

• JUNE 23 •

The Juggle Is Real

I try not to talk about struggle in my life these days, because I recognize that there are women and other individuals around me who truly are struggling—in their lives and for their lives. Many are struggling without much hope or much help. I do know what struggle is, and I struggled mightily during my periods of addiction and mental illness, domestic abuse, and self-induced harm. I have struggled with severe workaholism and cancer and self-doubt. I am exceedingly grateful that today I have the privilege of having to *juggle* through my life, rather than *struggle* through it. For the most part, the decisions I have to make and the activities that I engage in for my recovery and everything else are things that I have clear choices about, even though sometimes the choices feel overwhelming. I often find myself with too many balls in the air. Can you relate? When I start to feel like life is a struggle, I usually just need to eliminate a few balls, go back to basics, and return to my recovery practices. Sometimes I even have to let a few balls drop and roll away.

Life is a balancing act, a daily juggle of assessing what's important, doing it, and letting go of the less important things.

• JUNE 24 •

On Meditation

I once thought that I would need to have a strong and consistent meditation practice to be taken seriously in recovery. If you are a person who has that, much respect for you and your recovery. I'm still figuring it out. I have taken more than a few meditation courses, including a very expensive one. I have a bookcase filled with books on meditation, and I own two meditation cushions. Despite these things, I should accept that I may never be a model meditator and instead embrace who I am when it comes to meditation. Just like being in recovery, there is no one way to meditate.

I love to meditate and feel the benefits of meditating every time I do it. I like to meditate in all sorts of different ways, including walking meditation. I do sitting meditation, but more often in my recliner than on either of my cool meditation cushions. I like both silent meditation and guided meditation, and one of my favorite practices is sitting in the backyard meditating to birdsong. I love to meditate on the beach in a circle of women at sunrise. My meditation practice is erratic and inconsistent, but my appreciation for the practice is strong.

It's called a meditation practice
for a reason. Keep practicing.

Healthy Mutual Dependence

In her book *A Place Called Self: Women, Sobriety, and Radical Transformation,* Stephanie Brown, PhD, highlights a fascinating element of recovery, one that I have also spent a lot of time thinking about in more than three decades of recovery. Brown argues that in recovery, "*independence* involves a paradoxical acceptance of *dependence*—a sense that we can't and don't survive alone—along with an understanding that we ultimately stand alone." Practicing healthy, mutual dependence is about acknowledging and acting upon the need that we all have for connection with other beings. Out of those connections and related support, we learn to practice healthy ways of living that allow us to take responsibility for ourselves, and *that* turns into us creating our independent, autonomous, and separate selves. One of the taglines of the She Recovers movement is "You don't have to recover alone." For those of us who have experienced trauma, learning to rely on others as we regain our sense of self is difficult work. We approach it tenderly.

From I *to* we *and back to* me,
this is the brilliance of recovery.

• JUNE 26 •

Other People's Opinions

There's an anonymous quote that goes, "What other people think of me is none of my business." It took me a long time to learn that and to believe it, to embrace it, and to practice it. As women in recovery from any of the things, we often have low self-esteem and a lot of self-doubt. And I wasted years of my life worrying about what other people thought of me. I mostly thought that they thought badly of me, although I never had any evidence of that, and truthfully, they had no reason to think poorly of me. I can honestly say I don't worry about it at all today. I'm sure that some people do think various things about me. I can't say what they are or if the things they think are good or bad, right or wrong. It just doesn't matter.

The only opinion about me that matters
is my opinion of myself.

The Ripple Effect

If you have been in recovery for any period of time, you will have experienced the ripple effect. Basically, *the ripple effect* refers to how one particular action or event can lead to a series of other things or unintended outcomes. For example, I got into recovery at age twenty-seven because I really needed it, and when I was twenty-nine, I ran into a person (also in recovery) who would become my life partner. My partner and I introduced my sister to recovery when she really needed it, and she also ended up meeting someone in recovery with whom she has made her life and built a family. Today, the four of us lead full and happy but not perfect lives in recovery, and when our children and other loved ones have also needed recovery support, we've been able to provide it. I'm very proud of us. And I'm proud of you too. Choosing recovery (regardless of what you are recovering from) is one of the most profound things you can do in your life. You do it for yourself or you do it for the people you love, but you cannot begin to imagine how much of a ripple effect your recovery might have—not only in this lifetime, but for generations to come.

One good decision can change everything.

• JUNE 28 •

Extraordinary Mamas

Mothering can be hard in recovery. It takes a lot of stamina—and grace—to take care of ourselves as well as our little people when we are navigating a new way of being. And what about the women in recovery who are mothering children with high needs? My beautiful friend Payton is one such mama to a lovely young man with autism named Greyson. I know from Payton what a handful Grey can be, how difficult some days are. But I've also witnessed their sweetness together. Sometimes, when Payton and I are visiting over Zoom, Grey will wander over to her and plant a kiss on the top of her head, and I can see how that feels for her in her expression. It's heart-melting. I once said to Payton that I couldn't imagine how difficult life must be sometimes. She replied, "I don't think about it. It's my life; I just do it." And she is doing it, moving through each day loving Greyson and being loved by him. Payton and her son are beyond special, and I honor and love them both, exactly where they are.

Softness in the face of hard things
is something to behold.

Designing a Higher Power

I am a woman in long-term recovery, and I believe in a higher power that has nothing to do with organized religion. Most days my higher power is something related to the divine feminine; other days it's the ocean, an astonishingly beautiful sunrise, or something else in nature, and sometimes it's my dead mother. I learned early in my recovery that I didn't have to define my higher power but that I might benefit from believing that somewhere outside of myself there is an energy or force that I can tap into to feel comfort, to receive inner guidance, or to express gratitude. My concept of this higher power and what it brings into my life is dependable but malleable. Like everything in recovery, choosing whether to have a higher power (or not) or deciding what that looks like is completely up to us. Everything about this works for me.

Some days my higher power is a goddess;
other days it's a lilac bush. Both are valid.

Endings as Completions

We don't always have control over how and when certain things end, but we can control how we view and characterize most endings. I'm not referring to death here, but rather the endings of projects, jobs, relationships, friendships, and marriages. I think our first instinct is to think of endings as hard and painful, but they can also bring pride, satisfaction, and joy. A friend of mine recently shared some profound thinking about an important ending in her life—the end of her long marriage. She wondered aloud why it was that ending a long marriage had to be seen as something tragic. She preferred to think that ending her marriage was simply about completing something. Not a ruptured or destroyed or even broken marriage, just a beautifully completed story about two people who had created a family and were ready to move on to something else. Her thoughts made me think of the Dr. Seuss quote "Don't cry because it's over, smile because it happened." How do you feel about accepting that some endings are just natural and beautiful completions?

Beautiful things sometimes end
to make room for more beauty.

JULY

When New Life Brings New Life

I know a great many women who choose to recover from substance use issues for their children, and I honor them. I am also one of them. At age twenty, and with unending gratitude to a man I once thought was my entire reason for being (turned out he wasn't even close), I found myself pregnant. Ashley, the beautiful baby girl who came into the world on July 1, 1981, did more than change the course of my life—she saved it. That pregnancy—and the responsibilities of single motherhood—marked the beginning of my trying to stop using substances and become the mother I wanted to be. Working on stopping was the theme of my life for the first few years of that little girl's life. Successfully stopping didn't happen until she was six and my second beautiful daughter was two.

People say we can't recover for anyone else, that we must be driven by our own desire for recovery. I never wanted it for myself until I wanted it for my children, so I beg to differ.

Our children can inspire us to recover,
but the work of recovery is ours.

• JULY 2 •

Caring for Ourselves First

We've all heard the saying about putting on our own oxygen masks before trying to help someone else. I get how that is just the absolute best idea when we are on an airplane, but I am not nearly as comfortable embracing the concept in my everyday life. For those of us who dance with codependency, taking care of ourselves first is never our first instinct. It certainly never occurs to me to take care of myself first when a situation arises that involves something or somebody who needs taking care of. I find I need to be more proactive than reactive, which means carrying my proverbial mask into every aspect of my daily living and giving myself shots of oxygen throughout each day. I mean that quite literally sometimes—I need to stop and take deep breaths. Then, when the plane starts careening, I'm ready, not reacting. Audre Lorde said that caring for ourselves isn't about being self-indulgent; it's about self-preservation. She went on further to say that self-care is an act of "political warfare." I feel that.

Practicing self-care includes the regular act of taking deep breaths.

Adrenaline Seeking

Learning that I was addicted to my own adrenaline was a key moment in my recovery from workaholism. I used to think that adrenaline addiction could only apply to me if I were a compulsive participant in dangerous sports or daredevilish activities. Trust me, you will never find me jumping out of a plane or motorcycle racing. The adrenaline rushes that ruled my life, and the ones that I still must be on active alert about, are the rushes that come when I jump into yet one more project or try to barrel through two hundred emails in a few hours. I'm most at risk of a "lapse" or "relapse" into heightened overworking when I start feeling buzzed about having an extra-long to-do list. Extreme work or life pressure is no longer my fix for my adrenaline addiction; it's an indicator that I need to slow the hell down. If I don't, the adrenaline rushes will destroy more than my serenity; they will destroy my health. Trading out adrenaline seeking and calling in serenity seeking will be a lifelong journey for me. But my life will be longer for it.

Some of us get more kicks from
contentment than thrill seeking.

Embracing Our "Rawkward"

My sweet southern friend Dixie coined the term *rawkward* (raw + awkward) a while back. As Dixie explains, the term describes how many of us, especially those of us who are introverts, often show up in the world "rawkwardly." For Dixie, this is because the longer she is in recovery, the less capable she is of participating in small talk. Her tendency these days is to dive right into soulful presence, which, as she observes, can weird people out a little bit—or a lot. I've observed this too. The social comfort zone for so many is to talk about the weather, current events, the small details of our lives. The magic of conversation for me happens when I invite or am invited to connect more deeply. I prefer to share or ask questions about what is lighting up our lives, or what new things about ourselves we have learned, or simply how our heart is doing on any given day. It does feel "rawkward" to initiate or participate in such authentic conversation. Let's do it anyway.

I have too many big feelings and big ideas
to waste time on small talk.

On Inheriting Privilege

We can't control what family or circumstances we are born into, and I'm not so naive to suggest that we all land exactly where we are supposed to. We don't inherit opportunity in equal measure. It's not fair that there are people in my life who were born into poverty, racism, and other traumas beyond description. My dear friend Shari says that racism is the "compromising and minimizing" of her life solely because of her African American ethnicity and heritage. I hate that that is her truth.

I was born into a family whose traumas were buried deep but yielded mental health issues and addiction nonetheless, until some of us made the decision to heal. I inherited strength and resilience from my family of origin, which has helped make recovery possible, but I also inherited white privilege, which means that recovery is more available to me than to some others. It also means I have an obligation to use my privilege to do better and help others, or at least do no more harm.

We can't always escape what we are born into,
but if we are fortunate, we can decide
what we leave behind.

• JULY 6 •

Catastrophic Thinking

One of the most useful skills I've developed in recovery has been letting go of catastrophic thinking. Back in the day, when addictive behaviors and other unhealthy habits ruled my life, I always expected the worst to happen. I didn't have to ruminate on potential calamities for very long; I could jump to a worst-case scenario in a hot minute. I didn't know at that time that catastrophic thinking was not only a symptom of my anxiety disorder, but also a contributor to it. Of course, I didn't know I had an anxiety disorder, either.

I'm not saying terrible things never happened in my past, but roughly 99 percent of the horrible things that I envisioned happening did not. Today, I understand that playing out disastrous outcomes is irrational and a waste of time and energy. I prefer to stay in the moment as much as I can and hope for the best-case scenario. If things turn horribly wrong, I'll deal. One of the other things I've developed in recovery is an understanding that when bad things happen, I will always be supported to get through them.

I take deep breaths and remind myself
that most things work out.

• JULY 7 •

Through Our Eyes

We all have that friend who we think is just the bomb but who struggles with believing she is as great as we know her to be. We wish that she could see herself the way that we see her. That she would understand how important she is to the whole of our recovery community, how she brings something special and uniquely hers to the table. Her wit, her commitment, her realness. One of her superpowers is being transparent about how she feels about things, good or bad. She judges herself harshly for that sometimes, rather than viewing it as a badge of authenticity. Her generosity and willingness to serve and support the women recovering around her know no bounds, and we are all grateful for that and benefit because of it. We see her work so hard to support each member of her family, and we see that it tires her. But she's unstoppable when it comes to helping others. We wish that she could give herself the same level of care she provides to others, all the time. She doesn't, but we catch glimpses of her self-care now and then, and we sigh with relief for her. One day she'll believe in her own magnificence. We can't wait to see that day.

It's okay to believe in people before they believe in themselves. They will get there.

• JULY 8 •

Balancing Life and Work

Balancing life and work doesn't come naturally to me. Fortunately, I have figured out that I get to define *balance* for myself. As someone in recovery from overworking, I have to admit that balancing life and work doesn't look the same way for me as it might for most people. It doesn't mean working a certain number of hours per day followed by a certain number of hours living my life. Sometimes, I work a ten- to twelve-hour workday, and balance looks like taking off an entire Friday or a couple of afternoons during the week. Sometimes I work twelve days in a row and take a week off. This is what works for me.

Regardless of how my schedule shifts and how free I feel by managing it in my own way, I always need to be vigilant in tracking work versus nonwork hours and days. What I know for sure is that I tip over into the "more work than life" trap quite naturally. I may not achieve balance in my life easily, but I remain committed to having it, as I understand it, in my life.

Work less, live more. It's a worthy goal.

• JULY 9 •

Supporting and Being Supported

My friend Nona has shared in detail with me about how grateful she is to be part of a small group of four recovering women who text-support one another and have for years. They send texts to each other at different times of the day and, according to Nona, just about anything goes. They share pictures of everything, including children's graduations, weddings, a new pedicure, morning face in bed, haircuts, and even potential dates from dating apps. They share about books they love and Netflix shows they like, but more importantly, they reach out for help when they feel like they are falling apart. Nona says it sometimes feels easier to be honest in a text than in person, so there's that. They reach out for understanding and acceptance when one of them can't get out of bed because of depression, and they share advice when it's requested. If one of the four falls away from the group, someone else checks in with them. No one gets left behind. They all feel so grateful to have each other at the tips of their fingers, on their phone in their back pocket.

Who's in your back pocket? Can you cultivate a small friends' group so you are supported too?

• JULY 10 •

Be Yourself, Unapologetically

I think that recovery is in large part about getting to that place where we accept who we are so fully that we stop apologizing for who we aren't. Not that we claim perfection, but rather we live our lives knowing that our imperfections are what make us interesting and what make us unique. The brilliant actor Viola Davis is quoted as saying, "You can't be hesitant about who you are." Yet, we do hesitate, don't we? We don't always bring our full, imperfect selves to the party of life. Or when we do, we feel obliged to apologize for not being or doing enough—or, for some of us, for being too much. How many times a day do you say "I'm sorry" for something? No, seriously, I think you should do the count one day. And then reflect on how many times you said "sorry" because of something you believe you are or did that needed an apology. Write about it.

I'm sorry, not sorry. For being me.

For the Love of Reading

When I was in the first grade, my teacher pointed out to my parents that I was an incredibly bright reader for my age. I loved the attention from the teacher and my parents, as I recall, and I fell passionately in love with reading. I loved escaping into other people's stories and felt that I belonged there more than in my own family a lot of the time. My parents were proud of my reading prowess, which felt good, and they bought me a lot of books, which felt even better. I particularly loved books that were written in series, because I never wanted my connection to the characters in my books to end. By the time I was seven I had a full series of Bobbsey Twins books, and a few years later, most books in the Nancy Drew series. Agatha Christie mysteries were a favorite when I was only about ten. As a teenager, I branched out and came to love poetry, self-help, and self-development books, but my greatest passion has always been reserved for fiction. I still escape into other people's stories, but I love living in my own story best of all.

Who says we can't find friends
between the covers of a book?

• JULY 12 •

Recovery Dates

I am a strong believer in the concept that, in recovery, it's more important to make our days count than it is to count our days of recovery. But I also understand that counting days is a real motivator for some people. Fair. Still, I worry that the extreme focus on counting days in anonymous programs invites shame and guilt for people who break their recovery streak. I also respect that I'm not the boss of those programs. Plus, one of those programs saved my life, so there's that.

I personally have a few different dates. I went to treatment for alcohol, cocaine, and other substances in July 1987 and have not used cocaine or drunk alcohol since. That's one date. I smoked massive amounts of marijuana until May 1989, so there's my second. When my mom passed away in spring 2000, I took prescription drugs for a couple of days, so there's my third date. And in February 2011, I started my journey of recovery from workaholism. So many dates, right? Here's the thing: I consider myself to have been in recovery from the moment I decided to heal back in 1987. That's the date that means the most to me. I get to determine what my dates are and what they mean. And so do you.

One day at a time. That's the deal.

She

When she came into our circle for the first time, she was overcome with feelings, some familiar, others new. She came to us knowing that she was missing something in her life but lacking clarity on what exactly that was. She only knew that her loneliness was growing, and she felt sad and a little bit afraid a lot of the time. She longed, truly longed, for something that she couldn't even name, something that she knew was both inside of and beyond herself. When she first sat in our circle, she felt immediate anxiety as she heard others talk because even though we assured her that she didn't have to share, she knew she *needed* to, and the thought of having to speak the truth aloud terrified her. She felt amazement as others shared pieces of themselves that she sensed fit exactly into pieces of herself. Pieces that she had forgotten about for so long. And she felt hope. Hope that somehow she could find and share the words (when the time was right for her) and they would be received in the same way as she was receiving others'. Respectfully. Humbly. Gratefully. She hoped that she could be a part of whatever it was that was happening in that circle of women. She didn't know that she already was.

She recovers.

Obstacles

Everybody encounters obstacles in life. There are the structural or societal obstacles that are difficult to break through unless you have the right amount of privilege and power. There are also the health and genetic obstacles that we can't control. But what about the obstacles that we *can* control?

Usually, it's easier to recognize external obstacles or limiting forces outside of ourselves than to acknowledge the obstacles that are self-imposed or self-created. Insecurity and self-doubt are the biggest self-imposed obstacles that I've had to overcome. We can look at obstacles as signposts and indicators. We can observe them and be clear about them, but I've figured out the importance of not bulldozing or pushing through our obstacles. Rather, we can find a resting place to reflect and then design the best way forward. Sometimes obstacles are not meant to be overcome. I know this because I have been my own greatest obstacle throughout my life.

What obstacles do you face today? We may not be able to control all of them, but we can choose how we cope with them.

• JULY 15 •

Recovering on the Beach

Since 2012, I have had the great honor of facilitating women's recovery retreats on a beach in Mexico. Several times a year, for seven days and seven nights, twenty-two women come together to heal, grow, and celebrate our recovery journeys. The weeks are filled with laughter, tears, beach walks, yoga, and the most fabulous food. There's magic in the days of sun, sand, and sea that open with gatherings on the beach as the sun rises and close with an evening sharing circle. The women who attend are indeed a privileged lot, and they recognize that, but they too have traumas and heartache and yearn for connection with like-hearted souls. I love watching women remember or learn for the first time what it feels like to practice radical self-care, to be reminded that they deserve recovery and that they deserve such a nurturing, sacred pause. I love knowing that each one will return home renewed and passionate about her recovery, many with a new desire to help grow the recovery movement. I hope that you can join us one day or have a similar experience. The guacamole is to die for.

We all deserve to be cared for, instead of being the caregiver, occasionally.

• JULY 16 •

Make Room for Better

I don't know about you, but sometimes I hold on to things that are serving no useful purpose for much longer than I should. For some reason, I'm hesitant to get rid of the stapler that hasn't stapled in five years. The lacy jacket from my youthful disco days that won't fit me again in this lifetime. University textbooks from over three decades ago. Outdated ideas about whether size and weight matter (they don't). People I've outgrown. Expectations of others that I hold on to that only harm my heart. Some days I'm paralyzed by the number of extraneous things in my life, and I feel the world closing in on me. When I can't hear or see clearly because of all the noise and clutter, I know it's time to start turfing out elements of my life that are weighing me down. Self-care guru Cheryl Richardson shares, "If you eliminate what no longer works, you illuminate what does." What a brilliant concept. Let's go with that.

I need to remember that life is fuller when
I empty it of things that I don't need.

Adoption

At one of the retreats that my daughter and I hosted recently, there was a clear theme and thread about adoption among our beautiful guests. Over the course of four days and as many evening sharing circles, we listened to the tender and inspiring stories of two adoptees, a woman who had given up a baby daughter for adoption, and several women whose parents or siblings had been adoptees. The heartfelt sharing by the adoptees about yearning for the truth about their roots and the various ways they found it touched all of us. And then the woman who had given up a daughter at birth shared directly to the two women who had themselves been given up for adoption. She spoke to them about how profoundly broken her heart was when she handed over her little baby girl, and she articulated how deeply she still loved that baby and thought about her every single day. Those three minutes of healing connection between three women were some of the most powerful moments I have ever experienced in a recovery circle. Recovery is amazing.

We do recover. From gifting babies into adoption and being the babies who are adopted.

• JULY 18 •

Recovery Is a Process, Not an Event

I write and talk about how recovery is an ongoing process because it really is worth repeating. Take away the fact that our lives are complicated and that our healing unfolds layer by layer, and let go of the idea that we can change incredibly complex things about ourselves overnight, and you are left with several holy truths. The first holy truth is that recovery doesn't have an end point—for anyone. If recovery were a symbol, the infinity symbol would be appropriate. The second holy truth is that our recovery—our individual, unique experiences of healing and growth—expands and progresses on our own timelines. We can "be recovered" in some ways in our lives, but we're always recovering in others. Recovery is not a race, and we get to address the pieces that need attention when we determine the time is right for each piece. There will be important events taking place along our recovery journey, and many will be celebratory, but they are just markers of the journey, not the journey itself.

I am not sure where I am headed in the process,
but I'm excited to keep going.

Abandoning Ourselves

I have been abandoned by others emotionally, and it hurt like hell. It wounded; it was traumatizing. Trust was abused and lost, and that affected more than that one relationship with one person—it made subsequent emotional vulnerability a risky prospect. No matter whom we get to know, we'll never be immune from abandonment, because people are human. In retrospect, however, the most painful abandonment I've experienced is when I've abandoned myself. This has happened multiple times over the years.

Abandoning ourselves is an unconscious behavior, sometimes a response to earlier abandonment. Those of us in recovery have a long history of abandoning ourselves, but the good news is we can find ourselves bit by bit. We can earn back our trust in ourselves. We can be vulnerable again. Today, I have my own back; I stick with myself when things get rough. Even in the worst of times I tell myself, "It's okay, I'm here. I'm not going anywhere."

Self-abandonment doesn't have to last—
we can find ourselves again.

• JULY 20 •

Identifying Past Wounds

I don't always love the "digging around in our past" part of recovery. Most days, I crave and strive to be present and living in the now, or to be forward-thinking and forward-moving. When I do visit the past, my preference is to focus on the happy and good parts. But the wounded pieces of my past come calling without being invited. Completely new experiences and circumstances can trigger my very old, very core wounds. I've done a lot of therapy and have been working on my recovery for a long time, so when my core wounds are triggered, I can usually respond to them with gentle understanding. One of my predominant past wounds is abandonment, and it's amazing how often it shows up. It's even more amazing that I recognize it almost immediately, acknowledge it, feel it, and then remind myself that it's an old hurt. I remind myself that the only person who can abandon me now is myself, and I'm not about to ever do that again.

I greet my past wounds with understanding
and compassion, then I release them,
again and again.

There She Is

My daughter (and co-founder of She Recovers) Taryn spends a lot of time preparing themes for every yoga class she teaches at our recovery retreats. At one recent retreat, seeking inspiration, Taryn opened up Glennon Doyle's *Untamed: The Journal (How to Quit Pleasing and Start Living)* and landed on a page entitled "There she is." As Taryn reflected on what Glennon had to say about recognizing ourselves, she started to think about how that line felt for her. As she shared with her class, she remembered very clearly how one day in early recovery, she caught a glimpse of herself in a mirror and thought to herself, *There she is. I'm back.* As she shared that important moment with a yoga studio full of retreatants, Taryn shared that she, and others, often have those "There she is" moments when their lives slow down. I know that to be true as well. By the time most of us gift ourselves with any sort of retreat or time to ourselves, we are usually tired and burned out, but it only takes a few hours or sometimes a day or two of resting and being with ourselves, or with other women in recovery, to begin to recognize ourselves again. Those moments of seeing ourselves again are sacred, and we all deserve them.

I hope you catch a glimpse of yourself often,
or at the very least, one day soon.

In Honor of the Ones Who Came Before

As a student of women's history, I feel compelled to recognize and honor the pioneering women who came before me and paved the way for me to recover. This includes women like Marty Mann, who was the first woman and lesbian to achieve long-term sobriety in AA. She also advocated for better treatment for alcoholism and was the founder of the National Council on Alcoholism and Drug Dependence. I am also passionate about honoring the multitude of other remarkable women whose footsteps I follow in recovery. I'm talking about the women who showed up in recovery programs in the decades before I did who helped normalize and grow women's recovery communities, who created space for the rest of us to fall or step into when we were ready. Because they committed themselves to a recovery program—and stayed—I had a place to land when I was ready to start my own recovery journey. The number and nature of women's recovery communities has expanded, and each of us is taking our place in the unfolding of women's recovery history. I honor you for being a part of it. I honor all of us.

We are all pioneers in our own recovery;
we have a responsibility to be good stewards
of the recovery movement for those to come.

The Pressures of Purpose

I have very mixed feelings about the importance of all of us finding our purpose in recovery, especially when recovery is by definition its own purpose. I've had plenty of conversations with women who feel like purpose-seeking is an integral part of their healing journey. But I've also heard a lot of women talk about how they feel pressure to find purpose when really they just want to live a more balanced, happy life with the people they love. I think that the difference is largely in how we think about purpose; we've been conditioned to think that a life purpose has to be a big deal that is impactful for a lot of people. What if our purpose is simply to heal and be the best version of ourselves that we can be, to love ourselves and the people around us? My dear friend Jen Pastiloff has a beautiful quote that I think captures purpose perfectly. Jen says, "When I get to the end of my life, and I ask one final 'What have I done?' let my answer be 'I have done love.'" I can't think of a better way to think about purpose. Can you?

My purpose is to lean into each day
and live it the best way that I can.

Releasing Perfection

We aren't each born a perfectionist; we become one. The root cause of my perfectionism, according to more than a few of my therapists, is my desire for positive attention and my fear of disapproval. In childhood, I was expected to be perfectly behaved, perfectly clean and tidy, a perfect student. So I believed I needed to be a perfectionist if I was ever to achieve excellence. Everything was black and white—perfect or not. There was no gray area.

Such polarized perfectionist thinking perpetuates a cycle of fear of disapproval; feeling insecure, inadequate, not enough; and thinking about ourselves based on what we do, how we look, how we present. Regardless of whether we are expecting perfection of ourselves or of others, it doesn't usually yield good results. So today, I embrace the principles and practices of "good enough" and "close enough." Over and over again. I embrace the gray.

I love that I have learned how to release my perfectionism, at least some of the time. Imperfection isn't a problem; it's a human condition.

To be human is to be imperfect.

• JULY 25 •

Belonging in Community

Not long ago, I sat with a group of amazingly bright women contemplating the meaning of *belonging*, of finding community. We used different words to paint a picture of what belonging looked like, but at the heart of the matter, we were mostly saying the same thing. We started out by separating the word into its two component parts and pondered the brilliance of *longing* to *be* as an apt description of a sometimes-elusive concept. We wondered if belonging was simply the opposite sense of feeling untethered or disconnected. We weren't sure whether feeling like we belong to ourselves is a prerequisite for belonging or if feeling like we truly belonged somewhere is what leads us back to ourselves. As our friend Seanna so beautifully concluded, "Belonging lives as a seed planted in the deep, tender soil of our soul and grows there, wrapping its tendrils around our heart each time we create a core memory of being included, being seen, being held, or being loved."

May you belong to yourself, always, and may you find belonging in a community with healing and joy at its center. You deserve nothing less.

We Choose Our Responses

We can't choose what happens to us, what others do, what others say, or any circumstances that are external to our own control. But we can choose our responses. When something negative happens or I encounter something that I don't approve of or someone says something that I'm unhappy with, I try to pause and just take up space in that liminal moment. That moment in the transition—the moment between moments—can be very handy. It gives me time to breathe and consider. I've learned that there's a difference between responding and reacting. Taking time in the liminal space allows me to avoid the knee-jerk reactions that come as reflex.

There are consequences to our responses, just as there are consequences to our actions. Stephen Covey says, "Between stimulus and response, there is a place where we choose our response." Today, I choose to respond slowly, or at least that's what I will try to do. I'm not always successful, I admit. I sometimes skip to reaction, but then I have another choice—how will I respond to my reactionary response? Life gives me so many opportunities to figure these things out.

Recovery is made up of a series of responses instead of countless reactions.

You Are Here for a Reason

I share elsewhere how much I dislike the sentiment "Everything happens for a reason," but I can totally get behind the idea that we are all *here* for a reason. I don't pretend to know what those reasons are, most of the time. You are here, reading this entry on what is hopefully a lovely day in July wherever you are. I'm guessing that you are recovering from something in your life, which is what drew you to this book, and for some reason you thought to open the book to read today's entry. Maybe it's your fourth time through the book and you approach it differently each year. So while I've got you, let me remind you that you are indeed here for a reason. Let me remind you that you may not always feel like you belong in this world or in your life, that you might even feel unworthy of living it. It's important for me to remind you that even if life feels super hard right now, you are going to be okay. Please stay here, and if it hasn't revealed itself already, the reason or reasons you are here will one day become clear.

We may not know why we are here,
but we will learn in due course.

• JULY 28 •

Compassion for Self

I'm a very compassionate person. Especially when it comes to you. I can conjure up compassion for you in an instant if you make a mistake, if you appear to need help, if you have a bad day. You can be frustrated and angry, bail on a commitment, forget to do something you promised to do. You can be in dire pain, paralyzed, and unable to cope or show up. Regardless of your shortcomings or distresses on any given day, I'll pull out my most compassionate self to support you. I don't always find that same level of compassion for myself. I have to work hard to remember and then to follow up on treating myself with as much compassion as I would easily find for others. The best question I can always ask myself is "If this were someone you love, how would you practice compassion with them?" Then I remind myself that I, too, am worthy of that compassion, and I give it to myself.

I may have to dig a little deeper,
but I can find the same compassion
for me as I have for you.

• JULY 29 •

Grace

Anne Lamott is a wise woman in recovery and a brilliant writer. I love her beautiful quote "I do not at all understand the mystery of grace—only that it meets us where we are but does not leave us where it found us." In the Christian faith, grace is understood as a free and unmerited "favor" of god. I don't really identify as Christian at this moment in my life, but I'm comfortable crediting my own higher power with many of the times I've been touched by grace. I can see where grace has both given me new opportunities in life and changed everything about my life. Grace has, indeed, met me where I was. Finding recovery was a gift of grace, a beneficial accident. I wasn't looking for recovery, but someone in my life needed it, and, as a good codependent does, I embraced it in hopes that it would help him. He had no interest in recovery, but I kept exploring, and my life was changed forever.

Sometimes we only see how grace has touched our lives in retrospect. Perhaps we should look for it now.

Color Me Grateful

I don't know about you, but how I feel about color sure has changed since I've come into recovery. I used to be a person who colored my life in neutral tones and blacks. Beige, creams, and grays. My color tastes were rather "blah" because that is how I felt. Recovery brightened things up considerably. A few years into recovery, as my life became more vibrant, I started to embrace more vivid colors. This period included a rather protracted time when all of the décor in our house was made up of yellow sunflowers and forest green. I overdid it, and to this day I can't bear the sight of forest green outside of the forest. For more than a decade—and I suspect this will last for the rest of my life—my favorite color has been pale turquoise, with white and chocolate brown as minor but important accents. Those have become the She Recovers colors, but they are also very much what surround me in my She Cave (my basement, which is my very own space). If you search the internet, you will find that the color turquoise symbolizes calmness and clarity. How perfect that it's the color I've found to be most delightful in my recovery. Do you have a recovery color?

Color can be mood altering, in a healthy and most satisfying way.

Overidentifying

Very early in my recovery, a therapist asked me to tell her about myself, and I responded, "I'm an addict." I still remember the slight smile on her face as she responded, "Is that all you are?" Turns out, it wasn't. I was just used to underselling myself. There's no denying that I was addicted to substances and that addiction shaped my being. But I was and am so much more than my addiction, or addictions.

Over time, as a woman in long-term recovery, I have had the privilege and opportunity to develop a very full and complex notion of self. I am a mother and grandmother, a thought leader, a mentor, a friend, a partner, a writer, a consultant, an innovator. I can overidentify with any of those aspects of myself at times too, but I try not to. Today, I have closed the door on my identity as an addict, and I only use the term to introduce myself in Twelve Step meetings. I wish my therapist could see me now.

We can outgrow labels and shed identities, and we should.

AUGUST

Aging

I'm not sure that I ever looked forward to aging, but I've never been afraid of it or hated the idea of it. I'm just grateful to have made it this far. My mother never saw old age. I nearly died during my active addiction, then barely survived colon cancer. But it's more than gratitude. I'm excited to grow older. I'm ready to embrace my inner crone, even though I am not quite clear about when I'm allowed to call myself a crone.

Importantly, aging has been the invitation that I needed to make friends with my body. I've always thought that I had a nice face and good hair, but today I feel the privilege of growing older deep in my softening belly, in wrinkles that seem to multiply daily, in my often-aching muscles and my creaky joints and bones. Accepting my aging body allows me to be more fully me. A wiser and gentler me, but also a more radical and outrageous me. Aging is just another season in my life, and I'm here for it.

I think I might turn out to be
a very cool old lady.

On Privilege

I recognize that I access recovery services and support from a place of privilege. I self-identify as a white, cisgender, hetero, able-bodied, educated, feminist woman in recovery. I'm also Canadian, which means that in addition to being incredibly polite (you are probably familiar with the stereotype), I have access to health care and a supportive social safety net. My nationality is another form of privilege. Over the years, I have been the recipient of welfare, free addiction treatment (though that's not much of a thing in Canada anymore), and excellent universal medical care to get me through a range of health care crises, including addiction, depressive and anxiety disorders, and cancer.

Recognizing privilege does not place any blame on me as a recipient. But recognizing it means that when I view others who are not as privileged as I am, but who are facing similar challenges as I have, I understand that they are likely also facing additional challenges that I haven't. If those of us who are able to do so offer more help—or even remove barriers to accessing help—we can make a big difference in the lives of other women seeking recovery.

The first step is admitting my privilege—
what comes next is up to me.

Serenity by the Sea

I've always loved the ocean; any ocean will do. I was born near the Atlantic Ocean, I spend time each year swimming in the Mediterranean, and I now live on the edge of the Pacific Ocean in beautiful British Columbia. Before I leave this earth, I will dip my toes in the blue Aegean Sea.

My Pacific Ocean has various personalities that come and go with the sun and the storms. A wild, angry sea is just as captivating to me as a calm sea on a sweltering hot day, and, regardless of the weather, the beaches here feed my ongoing obsession to find the perfect piece of sea glass. We take our family to the beach to play, and a walk along the water with a friend is a soul-lifting activity. One of my favorite things to do, though, is to take myself to the ocean when I need to think. I have been known to take my troubles along, say a prayer at the water's edge, and release what I no longer need. The ocean—all oceans—feed my soul. Do you spend time by the ocean? What feeds your soul?

Deep oceans invite deep reflection.

Owning Our Part

Part of my recovery work—in the past and into the present—is to understand where I have done harm in situations or relationships. When I first got into recovery, my first instinct was to deflect and blame everyone but myself for all the messes in my life. After a while, I swung the other way and took ownership of and responsibility for more than what was mine to hold. I have since learned how to put situations in perspective and find appropriate balance. I have learned that there is a fine line between figuring out what our part is in any given situation and letting people off the hook who don't deserve to be set free. Today, I find it easier to own my own part when something goes sideways in my life or if I hurt another being through words or action. Recovery is about taking responsibility for our part in things, and I'm here for it.

I remain open to examining where my actions cause harm—to myself or to others.

Getting through before Letting Go

I used to preach that if something was troubling us, we just had to let it go. I believed that for myself, and I believed it for others too. If you shared with me that you had a deep resentment toward a friend or family member, I would tell you that you simply had to let it go. If I had a resentment or anything else that I invested a lot of emotional energy into, I'd tell myself that I just had to let it go. Unfortunately, the things that I thought I let go of never really went anywhere. They would resurface, and I'd have to let go again. And again. A few years ago, my daughter Taryn started to talk in her yoga classes about the idea that we must go *through* things before we let them go. A light came on for me listening to her words. As she reminded us, believing that we can just let go of things is a form of spiritual bypassing, as if we could avoid the bumper-to-bumper emotional traffic by going around the problem. I have since figured out that I need to sort out the energy behind the thing and resolve my feelings about it, and only then can I truly release it. Does this resonate for you?

Letting go is the end of a thought process,
not the beginning.

• AUGUST 6 •

The Power in Being Powerless

I completely understand and respect that many women have a problem with the concept of powerlessness that underscores Twelve Step recovery. Personally, I don't have a problem with the concept as long as I apply it in one very specific circumstance. In the program where I found recovery, the First Step reads, "We admitted we were powerless over our addiction—that our lives had become unmanageable." I felt a deep *hell, yes* the first time I heard and read that Step. As it was explained to me, the powerlessness came into play *if* or *when* I picked up the drug or behavior that caused me grief. And that was true for me: if I used substances, I had no control over what would happen next. I wasn't powerless over life in general, just over my addiction once I activated it. Because women have long known powerlessness, personally and historically, it makes sense that many are adamant about not assuming the idea of it regarding their own recovery. I think that's fair. I'm not here to suggest that you or anyone else needs to claim powerlessness to recover. I'm just here to offer an alternative understanding of the term so that we can all understand each other better.

My powerlessness kicks in when
I give in to my addiction. So I don't.

I Remember Her

I remember the me I used to be. The little me, lonely and bookish but also cute and fixated on being funny enough to make her mommy laugh. How she loved to hear her mommy laugh. I remember the teenage me. Confused and unprepared for the adult world that she found herself in when she fled from trouble at home only to land in trauma afar. I remember the new mother me, with a newborn in her arms and eventually another. I remember her finally settling into that place of true knowing that there were two delightful reasons to keep going, not in the same direction but down a new path. I remember early healing me, filled with wonder that she had survived and excited for the opportunity to thrive. I remember the maturing me, grateful to be on the other side of dysfunction and despair, ready to give her all to making the most of her remaining years. Ready to share a message of hope and to settle once again into a deep knowing that all would unfold as it is meant to. I remember the present me. Still bookish, never lonely, fixated on hearing the twinkling laughter of her own children and grandchildren.

I remember her. I hope I always do.

• AUGUST 8 •

Detaching

I've had to detach from a lot of things throughout my life. I've had to detach from people, situations, places. I've also had to detach from jobs, including one that I thought was my identity. I have had to detach from a lot of stories—stories that I told myself about myself, stories that turned out not to be true but had a huge impact on my life. Like the story that my parents didn't love me, perhaps the biggest story of all. I've had to detach from feelings in order to survive, to put aside my grief at times to care for my children. I've had to detach from other feelings that threatened to drown me at times. I've learned how to detach from other people's feelings and ideas, and I've detached from people. According to my friend Darlene Lancer, author of *Conquering Shame and Codependency* and *Codependency for Dummies*, sometimes it's about detaching from other people's "moods, actions, and words" so that we can "take our power back." I have taken my power back through detachment, and I'm keeping it.

Detaching is sometimes just about minding our own business, but other times it's about surviving our feelings and our lives.

• AUGUST 9 •

Acknowledging the Land

As a person who found recovery in a Twelve Step program, I am familiar with the concept of making amends and reparation where needed, not only in my personal life but as a member of society. Part of that for me is recognizing my privilege as a settler woman living on unceded territory. In the She Recovers community, we encourage members to learn about the land on which they live and include a land acknowledgment when they introduce themselves in our gatherings. We view such acknowledgments as a profoundly important practice, not a token gesture. A meaningful land acknowledgment requires us to do more than just recite the names of the original inhabitants of the land (using correct pronunciation). It requires us to understand the history of the land and recognize how colonialism impacted the Indigenous peoples where we now live. It is important for us to honor the land and people who lived here long before we did. As we continue to work on our recovery, we learn how we can make amends and reparation to the land where we live and to its first peoples. This is what recovery looks like.

I acknowledge with respect, gratitude, and humility the Lək̓ʷəŋən peoples on whose traditional and unceded territories I live, work, and recover.

The Best Is Yet to Come

I have long held as true that, for those of us in recovery from substance use or other addictions, one day the "must have that thing" switch flips, and we realize we no longer want the drink, the drug, the person, or the cigarette. There's plenty of work that goes into flipping that switch, but when it happens, it provides truly astounding relief. If it hasn't happened for you yet, keep doing the work. One day your switch will flip. And then one other day, perhaps many days later, you will realize that more than a few days have passed since you felt unworthy of the grace and the gifts that you are experiencing in your life. And you will think to yourself, "Wow. When did life get so good?" On that same day, you will start to wonder what else the universe might have in mind for you. You will get curious, and maybe even slightly nervous, about thinking that things might get even better. They will.

You may not always find it easy to picture
how good life in recovery can get,
but keep trying.

Finding Softness

It's hard sometimes to relax into softness. Harsh words and attitudes have been a constant in my life. I've been the recipient and the perpetrator of harshness. I know that I have a hard edge. Many don't see that edge, and it's not as hard as it used to be, but I know it's there. I have to practice being gentle. I have to soften into kindness. It sometimes takes a lot of effort and concentration.

I admire women who appear soft. I hang out with them to try to learn from them. So often, we don't want to be too soft or be called a softy, because people might take advantage of us. But I have to remind myself that finding softness isn't about giving up power or strength. My work is finding the *right amount* of softness, the *right amount* of tenderness. As I grow and age, I think it's getting easier. Finding softness can mean speaking less, holding back, being quiet. It's about the practice of finding softness with ourselves and others.

We can relax into softness by reminding ourselves that harshness is not our ally.

Many Pathways

The only recovery support that I was introduced to before I left addiction treatment was Twelve Step support. At that time, nobody talked or wrote about other ways of doing recovery, although of course there were other ways. I'm fortunate that Twelve Step recovery worked for me, and I loved it right from the start. I found my true self through working the Steps, I found a higher power, and heck, I even found my husband at a Twelve Step convention.

I still love my program of recovery, even though my recovery has gone in a lot of different directions recently. To be fully transparent, these days, I can go weeks or months without a meeting, but I love meetings when I get to attend. I don't have a sponsor or sponsees right now, but I'm still in close contact with many of the women I have supported or been supported by through the years. I haven't formally written a full set of Steps in a while, but I believe that I incorporate the Steps into my daily life. My recovery patchwork is tailored to my own needs, and yours can be too.

In recovery, choosing our own
pathway works best.

Outgrowing Drama

The period when I was actively using drugs and destroying my life was characterized by one drama after another, mostly of my own making. The same was true during my severe workaholism phase. There were also aspects of my life that were comedic, thankfully, but drama reigned on most days. Not unexpectedly, being enfolded in drama so much of the time was exhausting for someone already tired out from addictive behavior.

In recovery, we eventually lose the desire to seek out, create, or participate in drama. It's not an easy transition. For many of us, family dramas played out on the regular in our homes. When drama is the baseline reality of our lives, we naturally gravitate toward it because we aren't comfortable living without it. As our feelings and our circumstances regulate in recovery, our tolerance for high drama is lowered and lowered again. We stop creating it in our lives, and we learn to walk away from it when others create it for us. One of the hallmarks of strong recovery, in my view, is the absence of drama.

We outgrow drama when we
recover and heal.

Dear Seventy-Year-Old Me

I'm making my way toward you, and I'm not going to lie: I'd really like the journey to slow the hell down. I think of what and who I will be by the time I'm seventy. I hope that I'm wiser. I hope that I'm healthy. I hope that I have found even more serenity than I have now.

I hope I can look back and see all the people I've helped—and still be in touch with them and those who've helped me. I hope I have given much, but not so much that I've fallen into the trap of my old codependent ways. I hope that I am still spending time with women in recovery, women who are my age, and older and younger. We will need each other then just as much as we do now.

I hope that my work life has slowed down, that I'm finding more time to travel and to play with my grandkids. I hope I've learned how to play something on the piano or paint with watercolors. I hope that I'm still devouring books—and writing them. But most of all, I hope that when I get to be me at seventy, I'm just as content to be myself as I am now, all these years earlier.

As I age, who I am is more important than what I am.

Old Friends

When I was about ten years old, a very nice girl I met at camp gave me a book with a poem in it that said something like "There are gold ships and silver ships, but the best ships are friendships." That has surely turned out to be true in my life. I am rich in the number of close, long-term friendships I have formed in my life, starting in my youth and continuing through my troubled young adult years into today. My closest "old friends" are loyal and supportive and never abandoned me, not even during those dark times when I was abandoning myself. Throughout the difficult years, we still managed to co-create a lot of hilarity, light, and joy. Our shared history means so much, and although years can sometimes pass between visits, our memories and the care we have for one another act as the glue that binds our friendships together. I hope you have at least one old friend who knew you when. If not, perhaps you can think of somebody to reach out to for a reintroduction.

Old friends are among life's
most precious gifts.

• AUGUST 16 •

Creativity in Recovery

We don't have to be artists, authors, or silversmiths to explore the joys and benefits of creativity in recovery. Creativity is about applying ideas and effort to create something new; it's about enhancing expression. Others in my life are incredibly creative quilters, cooks, jewelers, musicians, and artists in many other realms. I still struggle to refer to myself as creative outside of my writing, but over my years in recovery, I have expended considerable effort on things like beading, knitting, crocheting, adult coloring, and a touch of interior design. Above all else, my own creative outlets are integral pieces of my mindfulness practice, but they also connect me to creatives in my past and present. The click of knitting needles calls in memories of my mom and grandmother. Today, beading with a group of women grounds me and brings me joy, as most of the bracelets I create are for other women in recovery. Recovery is all about exploring what brings us joy. What are your creative outlets?

Creativity allows us to take care of and express ourselves in new and illuminating ways.

• AUGUST 17 •

Owning Your Recovery Patchwork

It's essential, as individuals, that we truly believe that our chosen recovery pathway and patchwork is the very best one for us. If we don't, we'll find it hard to stay engaged with and invest in our recovery approach. We should be able to speak confidently about the modalities that we follow on our healing journey, which is easier to do when we have to put together our own recovery road map. We shouldn't allow anybody to dissuade us or make us think less of our choices, and we shouldn't try to convince anyone else that our way should be theirs. Our patchwork, as different as it might be, can never threaten anyone else's recovery. As Charlotte Kasl, author of *Many Roads, One Journey: Moving Beyond the 12 Steps,* wrote, "Neither I nor anyone else can take away someone's program by speaking of other ways. When someone thinks I can, it is because they have not internalized their own belief system and are giving their power to another person." I hope that you have internalized your belief in your own recovery.

May your confidence in how you do recovery sustain and empower you.

• AUGUST 18 •

Underscheduling

One of the affirmations from the Workaholics Anonymous program is "My life is full and underscheduled." It means that though we are doing things in our life, we allow for some open time and flexibility. I think that this is a concept we could all benefit from embracing in our lives, regardless of whether we are scheduling work or other daily activities. When I read or hear the term *underscheduled*, it conjures up ideas about time left over, time to spare, spaciousness, time to play. Underscheduling doesn't happen naturally for many of us; it requires intentional focus and action. I'm not always very good at underscheduling, but I try. I purposefully try to leave open gaps in my daily schedule. The gaps provide opportunities for me to rest or refocus throughout the day, to stop and stretch, hydrate, or take a walk. Those openings also allow me to attend to things that come up unexpectedly with more ease and less anxiety. Creating broad margins in my daily plans means purposely saying no to things, which isn't easy for an overdoer like me. Like anything in recovery, it takes practice to underschedule.

Learning how to create space in lives
that are usually overscheduled takes time,
but it's time well spent.

The Cult of Busy

In *Breaking Up with Busy: Real-Life Solutions for Overscheduled Women,* Yvonne Tally writes, "Once a seemingly innocuous habit, busyness is now a culture, an addictive attraction promising the opportunity to fit in, get ahead, and be the best." Tally suggests that breaking up with our busyness requires us to ask ourselves a lot of questions, including one that really struck a chord for this recovering workaholic: "What is the price of your pace?" The price of being overbooked and overscheduled is always going to be too high for me. I now much prefer a snail's pace to the frenzied pace I used to keep when I thought my only value was in what I did, not in who I am.

What is your relationship to busyness? Do you engage in it as a behavior? Is being busy a regular refrain in your vocabulary and maybe even a part of your identity? There's nothing to be ashamed of if the answers to the above questions are yes, but it is something to be aware of. When we know better, we do better.

We release our attachment to busy and find fulfillment in a slow but steady pace.

• AUGUST 20 •

Post-Traumatic Growth

My friend Jennifer Storm is a woman in long-term recovery from addiction and a sexual assault survivor, advocate, and internationally recognized victims' rights expert. When she speaks and writes about the horrific things that happened to her when she was a child and young woman, she does so from a place of post-traumatic growth, which refers to the remarkable growth and change that people can experience following highly traumatic life events. Jennifer's story is very much about finding hope in the aftermath of trauma and addiction. It's also about reclaiming or rewriting our stories. As she wrote in her book *Blackout Girl: Tracing My Scars from Addiction and Sexual Assault*, "Neither your pain nor your offender gets to finish your story. You have the power to write your ending." Her reminder that we have agency in how we heal and what we do afterward is an inspiration for all of us who have been victims of violence and/or sexual assault.

Few of us avoid trauma in our lives;
may we all experience growth
in the aftermath.

• AUGUST 21 •

Owning Mistakes

I'm not ashamed to admit that I screw up sometimes. But I must also admit, I'm not always super quick on the draw to take responsibility for my errors, omissions, mistakes, or misdeeds. I generally spend a bit of time thinking through how something is more your fault, or their fault, or anybody else's fault but mine. It's not fun to admit when I mess up. Unfortunately, owning my mistakes is the only pathway I know to releasing them. So I eventually exhaust the blame game and find my way into what is truer—that because I am human I made a mistake. I have to embrace the icky feelings that come along with screwing up, but then I claim the screwup and figure out how to get to the other side of it. Not everything can be fixed, but I can apologize for everything and try to avoid making the mistake again. And then I can move on.

Life can be messy for us humans,
and mistakes are a part of it.

• AUGUST 22 •

Retreating

All women deserve to retreat, to withdraw from everyday life to recalibrate, even if only for a few hours here or there. I have had the privilege of participating in and hosting women's recovery retreats for many years. *Privilege* is the key word here. Although formal retreats are not accessible to everyone, the concept of retreating has its origin in some very simple and affordable principles. Retreats can be about quiet time alone, about connection with like-hearted women, or a combination of both.

I encourage you to find a few hours, a day, a weekend, or a week and plan a sacred pause. You can create a retreat sanctuary in your home or your yard if you can't get away. Rest. Reflect. If you need the time to figure out what is working in your life and what needs to change, you can do that too. But the emphasis should be more on self-care than self-development while retreating; retreats are not workshops.

Retreating is my gift to myself.
Because I'm worthy.

Unknowable

There is something completely unknowable about the power of connection for women in recovery. I witness the healing that takes place when someone shares her hopes, her desires, or her innermost fears or traumas, and another woman nods in understanding. I see the connection; I feel it. The power of *me too* is indescribable, as we have all learned in recent years. I understand the psychology of spiritual support, that when we offer genuine compassion, encouragement, and reassurance, people feel safer to explore and experience their own healing. I know that we can support people verbally and with nonverbal cues. It all makes sense in my head. But I cannot and may never be able to explain how and why connection can bond us women in recovery together so *deeply* and so *quickly*. I can't think my way through to an understanding of the magic that often happens when circles of women gather in recovery. And I'm okay with not knowing exactly how and why it happens. I'm just grateful that it does.

Some things about recovery will always be a mystery to me. I am still grateful even in my unknowing.

• AUGUST 24 •

In Thanks and Forgiveness

When I first got into recovery, I used to think about the *her* I used to be, and all I could do was judge her. I'm over that now. If I could go back and visit with her now, I'd mostly just want to thank her for some things and tell her I forgive her for others. I'd thank her for being a loyal and loving daughter to her perfectly imperfect parents. I'd tell her I forgive her for running away from home at sixteen because things were hard at home and because she knew she was veering down a path that she didn't want her family to witness. I'd thank her for doing her best to survive leaving home without having been taught any adult survival skills. I'd thank her for saying yes to having the baby girls who gave her a reason for living and a reason to recover. I'd thank her for keeping her heart open all these years to all that life and recovery has to offer, especially knowing that open hearts get hurt. I'd thank her for who she is today, and I'd forgive her in advance for all the ways she may still screw up. Because she is sure to mess up a few more times yet.

Thank you. I forgive you.

• AUGUST 25 •

Going First

When asked why she shares so openly about her struggles, our friend and author Nadia Bolz-Weber says she hopes to help create a space for others to step into and feel safer admitting things about themselves. It's a form of leadership that she refers to as "Screw it, I'll go first." And she has certainly gone first in a lot of different areas. In addition to having written three *New York Times* best-selling memoirs, Nadia is a woman in long-term recovery from substance use, an ordained Lutheran pastor, and founder of House for All Sinners & Saints in Denver, Colorado, which is described on its website as "a liturgical, Christo-centric, social justice-oriented, queer-inclusive, incarnational, contemplative, irreverent, ancient/future church with a progressive but deeply rooted theological imagination." It's hard not to be inspired by Nadia and her work, and I like to think we have a few things in common. I have also embraced the "Screw it, I'll go first" idea—by being the first person in my family in generations to embrace substance use recovery. And although I didn't establish a church, I did—along with my daughter Taryn—create a pretty amazing recovery community. I doubt I will ever be as cool as Nadia (did I mention her tattoos?), but I'm incredibly honored to know her.

Somebody has to go first, but let's take turns.
How have you gone first?

• AUGUST 26 •

My Mother's Words

One of the things that most sustains me in my grief recovery, and in my recovery overall, is that even after several decades of missing my deceased mother, I still speak to her often. Before she died, she and I grew quite close (thank you, recovery), and so it's not too hard to envision what she would say to me during those times when I really need her. I talk to her about all the good things that are going on, as well as the bad or scary stuff. I love to imagine what she would think of the world as it unfolds around us and how she would respond to the changes in our family, the lovely changes and the harder ones. When I'm stressed or worried about something, I can hear her saying to me, "Oh, Missy—you know what you need to do, just do it." Or, "Just you never mind, you'll be okay." On the days that I miss her so much that I ache, I listen extra hard with my heart, and I hear her say the things that didn't come easily to her when she was alive, although I know she felt them. "Sweet girl, I love you and I'm proud of you." Thank you, Mom. I love you too.

Reparenting myself with words I give my mother is part of my recovery journey.

Better Late Than Never

The concept of "Better late than never" perfectly suits recovery. Yet I hear so many women express worry that it's too late and too hard for them to recover. I agree on the latter; it can be hard to make big changes in our life, especially if we are older. But I also think that all time matters, and if we can make positive alterations in our life even for a day, week, month, or year, we should choose that. I've seen people totally transform their lives with something they do over the course of just one day in recovery. I've seen women find such satisfaction and joy in just a year of recovery that it makes up for years and years of pain or dysfunction in their lives and the lives of their families. If we subscribe to or embrace the concept that every single day of our life matters, then showing up for each one consciously and with our full potential will never be too late. We will be right on time.

It's never too late to choose wellness,
regardless of our age or stage of life.

Walking the Labyrinth

My dear friend and recovery coach extraordinaire Kathy Robbins has a passion for designing labyrinths for women in recovery to walk. A labyrinth is an ancient, sacred space, a meandering set of passages that can be seen as a metaphor for our life's journey. When we physically walk the labyrinth, we enter an opening, follow a pathway that leads into a center, and then turn and retrace our steps until we are back at the beginning. We can't get trapped or lost in a labyrinth, unlike a maze. Kathy always invites us to walk the labyrinth quietly and slowly, turning inward, calming our mind, and remaining open to receive divine guidance. For those of us who like a little more direction, she tells us to focus on the four *r*'s of walking the labyrinth: remembering who we are, releasing anything getting in the way of who we are, receiving guidance and blessings, and returning to the world with a renewed sense of self, joy, and purpose. It's an experience to be savored. Much like life.

We don't come out of walking a labyrinth in quite the same state as we go in.

• AUGUST 29 •

Walking the Talk

I am someone who recovers out loud—proudly and consistently. I'm a talker, and I talk a lot about what recovery is broadly and how many ways there are to recover as well as how important it is to have agency in how we recover. I also talk plenty about what recovery and healing look like in my life, specifically. Like you, I have plenty of ideas about what I need to do to keep healing, and I try mightily to match my actions to those thoughts. Although I don't think of myself as a "say one thing, do another" type of person, I am a person whose reality stops short of my ideals. There was a time in my life when what I talked about doing rang empty, and my word meant little, so I had some work to do to gain back trust from others and regain a sense of personal integrity for myself. I've done that work, and I've become a person who walks the talk because my talk focuses on my imperfection. I will keep talking and walking. One step at a time.

Speaking our truth and then
walking in it takes practice.

• AUGUST 30 •

Living on the Edge of Our Best Life

Do you ever feel like you are on the edge of . . . something? Something good, maybe even exciting, but completely unknown? It's a great feeling, and it doesn't happen by accident. When we work on healing our past and intentionally live in the present while holding a bright vision for our future, things just start to feel like they are coming together. Living in a hopeful place invites anticipation; we anticipate that things are coming together and starting to integrate into something that looks like more of a whole. For some of us, this vortex of pride, gratitude, and excitement for what is to come can be described as a spiritual awakening—no religion required if that's not your jam. We just start to feel more fully "spirited" and alive. I've learned to lean into this incredible feeling and make the most of it. Not to spoil the plot, but these feelings do pass . . . yet they return again and again if you stay committed to your recovery. And each time we have the choice to stay on the edge of possibility or jump right into the abyss of what awaits us. Too scary? Well, the good news is we will be jumping in with you.

Perched on the edge of possibility, we have the option to go deeper and do better.

• AUGUST 31 •

Overdose Awareness

Overdose Awareness Day is a global event commemorated every August 31. It was created in 2001 by Sally J. Finn from the Salvation Army in Melbourne, Australia. It's the world's largest campaign aimed to end overdose, reduce stigma, and acknowledge and mourn those who have died, as well as honor the grief their loved ones feel. Our community, the She Recovers community, participates in the worldwide campaign to help raise awareness of the tragedy of overdose death and to educate people on how to prevent overdose. One year, we asked members of our community what they would say to someone who is currently at risk for overdose through their substance use disorder. Their messages were heartfelt and helpful, and included things like *People love you; you matter. Don't ever give up. Find your people and your support system, and keep them close. Keep Narcan close if you use opioids, and please know you are worth life and love! There is so much for you to do in your life, and you have a purpose. You are so important and so worthy of love and kindness.* I hope those messages landed then, and land now, for all who need them.

Stay here with us. It is possible to recover.

SEPTEMBER

Choosing Recovery

Recovery happens more often by choice than by chance. I do know a few people who, by some happy accident, ended up in the middle of a group of recovering people and basically thought, *Huh—seems like this might be something that I need too.* Clearly, there are not a lot of such people. Most of us, I believe, are very intentional about choosing to recover. We might come to it grudgingly, and we might go back and forth on it, but, ultimately, we make the decision to try recovery and then act upon it.

When I chose recovery, I was choosing to live. I don't believe that I would have survived much longer had I not made this choice.

I work hard every day to ensure that more women know that recovery is something that they can choose too. I think all the time about the people we have loved and lost before they chose recovery. I know some who made the choice but just didn't follow up and act on it soon enough. Every choice has a consequence. And sometimes that consequence is life.

I chose recovery long ago, and I
choose it again every day.

• SEPTEMBER 2 •

This Ends Here

We are the cycle breakers, you and I. It might not be the role we thought we would end up in, but here we are. We are breaking the cycle of addiction or some other dysfunction. If we are parents, our children will not have to witness or experience some of the things that we did. We do a lot of what we do for those we love, those who will come after us. They're worthy. This ends here.

Parent or not, you are a model for all the people you encounter in your life, even people you do not know. You don't even have to say anything; people will see and experience you as a person who makes good choices for yourself and your life. Of course, not everyone will appreciate the changes you have made or the boundaries you set as you change. Some may see you, your health, and your recovery as a threat to their own position in the cycle of dysfunction. Some may not see you at all, because they can't or won't. And still, this ends here.

Unhealthy patterns end with us.
For us and for those who follow.

The Imperative for Other Options

I was fortunate to find a recovery program that worked for me when I started my substance use recovery. However, it didn't take long for me to figure out that "my" program didn't work for everyone. Back then, if Twelve Step recovery didn't resonate for women, they couldn't usually find other supportive recovery options. I would get sad and worried about women whom I really came to love when they would start to distance themselves from the meetings that had stopped working for them. When they "left" the program, they left with no information about where else they could heal, what else they could do to keep recovering.

I'm happy to say that I know a lot of women who figured out how to recover on their own, even twenty-plus years ago. But some women felt alienated by their experience in Twelve Step recovery and isolated outside of it, and some of them returned to using substances. I lost a lot of friends simply because they were never told that there were other options for them to recover.

We must be supported to find and
follow individualized pathways and
patchworks of recovery.

Early Intervention

For the first decade or so of my recovery from a substance use disorder, I believed that recovery only happened after people hit rock bottom. As I listened to people in Twelve Step meetings share their descent into the hell of addiction, I somehow picked up that people were only motivated enough to seek recovery after they had lost their dignity, relationships, health, jobs, and worse. This message (and reality) remains true for many individuals, and we need to respect that. But it isn't true for everyone.

We need to talk and write more about early intervention. Addiction and mental health issues present and progress along a continuum. As much as we need to be here for the women who do hit a hard bottom, we also need to go upstream and help women who are struggling before things blow up in their hearts and their lives. I've made peace with how my own multi-bottomed story played out, but I sometimes wonder what my life would have looked like if somebody had noticed me struggling sooner.

Life is fuller and better when
help comes earlier.

• SEPTEMBER 5 •

We Are the Evidence

As a researcher and writer working in the areas of mental health and addiction, I know what to look for in the literature. I know how to study what recovery looks like on paper and in studies. I know what the indicators are for most addictive behaviors, and I know what the evidence base says about how to address them.

But even without my degrees and my expertise, I know what recovery looks like. It looks like me. It looks like you. Our co-occurring disorders. Our intersectionalities. Our family histories. Our shared experiences as women. Our different experiences as women. Our fears. Our victories. Our bright futures.

We are the evidence. I'm the evidence. You are the evidence. We are the evidence that recovery can be messy. It can be hard. It can be funny. It can make us cry. We are the evidence that recovery is something to celebrate. We are living proof that recovery happens.

Our experiences are valid—
we are our own experts and evidence.

• SEPTEMBER 6 •

Unbecoming

Glennon Doyle has said, "Recovery is an unbecoming." I love that. There are many definitions of *unbecoming*. One is an adjective that means "not flattering, fitting, suitable, or appropriate." Or it can be a verb that means "unraveling, investigating and solving something, understanding or explaining our beliefs." Sometimes, it's an undoing. Other times, it's exploration and slow unwinding of layers. In some cases, unbecoming can be perfectionistic, harsh, critical.

The process of becoming includes unbecoming the person we thought we were. Unbecoming who society thought I should be, who I thought I had to be, who my friends needed me to be. It's about unbecoming someone who is dependent on substances or work or the approval of others to become someone who is self-reliant in her recovery. We can begin unbecoming and then start the process of becoming, or maybe we start becoming first. It's a cycle; it's not linear. We don't have to fully unbecome to become.

Who will you unbecome
so you can become you?

• SEPTEMBER 7 •

Secrets

I have a confession. For as long as I've been in recovery, I've disliked the saying "We are as sick as our secrets." I don't like to describe myself as sick, and I think that the saying implies that we can or should share our secrets freely. I get it that secrets can eat away at us, but there's a reason why we've kept them secret for so long. Sharing a secret with someone close to us can provide relief, but talking about certain secrets may also require professional support. People have to earn the right to hear your secrets. Or my secrets.

My friend, actress and author Mackenzie Phillips, says that we don't have to uncover and disclose all of the *details* of our secrets. They can stay unexcavated. We don't even have to tell them to ourselves. We don't have to speak or share all secrets. But what I will tell you is that some secrets lose their hold on us only when they are shared. Uncovering our inner secrets can be about unlocking freedom. At least that's what it was for me.

I don't have any secrets today;
sharing them has helped me heal.

• SEPTEMBER 8 •

Our Grandmothers' Prayers

Spiritual writer Lalah Delia once tweeted, "Your grandmother's prayers—are still protecting you." What a comforting thought that is for some of us. In our She Recovers community, we talk often about our wounds passed on through intergenerational trauma, but we also celebrate our intergenerational wisdom and growth. One of my grandmothers happens to have been very religious, and I know that she prayed for me and all her family members every day. She's been gone for just over forty years, but the thought that her prayers—sent out into the universe as they were—still surround me fills me with both comfort and awe. This sentiment reminds me that the words and the thoughts and the energy that I put out into the world will still affect and protect my grandchildren too. I hope that my love for them is felt by them, their children (should they have any), and every generation that follows.

Even if you aren't the praying type, knowing that
the wishes that your ancestors wished for you
still surround you is an interesting concept.
Don't you agree?

An Invitation

Over thirty years ago, I accepted an invitation to recover from my addiction to substances. It was the right move. I feel a lot of gratitude for the opportunity to recover, and even more than that, I sometimes think that I'm a bit of a freaking miracle. You may be one too. I wonder sometimes why I was able to survive my deadly condition when so many others have not. Do you wonder that too? My living gratitude is to ensure that other women know the invitation to recover is there for them too. Not that we need to fully host their recovery if they accept the invitation, but that we can share all we know about the ways there are to recover and then invite them to get curious about what will work best for them. Sometimes we need to recognize that they aren't ready to accept the invitation to explore recovery. That doesn't mean they won't be ready one day. Invitations as such need to remain open-ended. We don't know when others will reply, "Yes, thank you—I'd love to join you."

Accepting an invitation to recover
can be hard the first few times.

• SEPTEMBER 10 •

Defining Recovery

There is no universal definition of recovery. Researchers, advocates, behavioral health professionals, and those of us with lived and living experience have never come up with one that we all agree upon. I happen to think that not having a solid, static definition is a good thing. It opens the door to empower us all to create individualized and diverse definitions for our own recovery, and it's a reminder that recovery differs across populations, cultures, and settings. Broadly speaking, recovery is a lifelong journey that takes time, looks different for each person, and may have many starts and stops along the way. I don't think we need to define it more than that, do you?

Recovery is . . . a practice.

Gone Too Soon

I am always devastated when I hear about another woman who has died from addiction or mental illness. That overdose deaths have increased exponentially in recent years due to a tainted drug supply has not numbed me to the tragedy that every loss of life from addiction represents. Whenever a young person, in particular, dies from addiction or mental illness, everybody always talks about how they are "gone too soon." We hear it over and over again. I think and say it myself, a lot.

Of course they're gone too soon.

They are gone too soon because they are young, and they are gone too soon because we needed more time to let them know we cared; we needed more time to try to help. We so often have regrets about loved ones dying before we were able to do or say something, so we need to act as if there is no tomorrow. Except I don't mean in the old way we used to think about it when we were using drugs or drinking. It's more about asking ourselves what we would do for and say to that person today if we didn't have tomorrow? And then we need to say and do it.

I'm thankful to have survived addiction and mental illness. I wish that everyone could.

• SEPTEMBER 12 •

Showing Up in My Recovery

Some days all that I've got to give others in recovery is my presence. Being a mature woman (well, in years anyway) with many decades of recovery behind me, I know that sometimes people expect that when I open my mouth in a recovery meeting or gathering, earth-shattering wisdom will come out. Although I think I do have some interesting—maybe even important—things to share about recovery occasionally, it's not because I'm older or have been doing things longer; it's because all of us in recovery are interesting and important. We show up for each other so that we can hear what we each have to say, because all of our words have meaning, and our stories are for sharing. One of my favorite things to do is attend a recovery meeting (like a She Recovers meeting online or an in-person She Recovers Sharing Circle or a Narcotics Anonymous meeting) and say nothing. Not raise my hand. Respond, "Thanks for asking, but I'm just going to listen. Thank you." Then I settle into being present, listening to all the wisdom that others have to share.

Showing up in humility is an indicator of growth in recovery.

To Step or Not to Step

I think that Twelve Step recovery worked for me because it provided a linear, straightforward road map for what I needed to do to reclaim my dignity and my life after I entered recovery. When I started my healing journey, I needed direction—I had few ideas of my own about how to move forward, and I didn't exactly trust myself or my instincts yet. I am still very grateful for the Twelve Step program that helped breathe life back into me, but there are other "step" frameworks out there that I am also drawn to. Charlotte Kasl's 16 Steps for Discovery and Empowerment provide one such powerful model, designed to help women address their mental, physical, and spiritual well-being. I love the first step in Kasl's model, which reads, "We affirm we have the power to take charge of our lives and stop being dependent on substances or other people for our self-esteem and security." Affirming that I have the power makes me feel strong and confident, ready to move forward into awareness and healing. Does that language resonate for you too?

Taking the first step of any recovery program can be life-giving; have you found a framework that works for you?

• SEPTEMBER 14 •

Unity over Uniformity

One of the philosophical pillars of the She Recovers movement is the idea that we have to be supported to find and follow individualized pathways and patchworks of recovery. This was not a concept that was apparent anywhere in my first decade of recovery. Individuals in or seeking recovery are very fortunate today to have so many different options for embarking on their healing journeys. And as options increase, people from all of the different corners of the recovery universe are starting to understand how important it is to focus on unity over uniformity. The most helpful thing to do when speaking with a person who is new to recovery from substance use or any other maladaptive coping behavior is to present them with the long and growing list of things they can do to figure out how and where they want to recover. No one group, organization, or program has a monopoly on healing, and we all have a responsibility to share freely about those modalities that might not be for us but may well save somebody else's life. When we want uniformity, we need to check our egos and ask ourselves why we think we get to determine what anybody else's recovery looks like.

We are stronger together, always.

Comfort amid Chaos

Chaos still shows up in our lives, even when we've stopped creating it ourselves. We don't have to attach to other people's chaos. We can remove ourselves, mentally and physically. We stop, breathe, and ask ourselves, "What is one thing I can do to disengage from the chaos and return to comfort?" Sometimes we find our comfort in a cup of tea, or in meditation or yoga. We might go for a walk or a run, or we might attend a meeting online or in person. At other times, a person or a pet is the comfort we are seeking to help escape the chaos. We hug our little people or our pups, or we reach out to someone who we know will be a soft landing place for us. We tell that person what is going on as a way of trying to release it. We ask them to remind us how we have successfully escaped chaos in the past. Because we have escaped it in the past. Our recovery is our evidence.

I detach from chaos by tapping into the peace and comfort that I know exist at my core.

• SEPTEMBER 16 •

Recovering Out Loud

I don't know about you, but my recovery started when I spoke the truth aloud. Speaking it aloud to somebody else gave it flight, lifted it up and away. Recovering out loud might mean you tell just one person that you are in recovery from suicidal ideation, depression, anxiety, or substance use. It doesn't mean you have to start an international movement. It doesn't mean that you reveal your recovery on social media or the front page of the local newspaper. It might just mean that when somebody around you is talking about a personal struggle or something a family member is going through, you turn to them and say, "I have some personal experience with that. Do you mind if I share?" When you do share in this way, you will be helping one another and also helping to eliminate stigma.

Here's the thing: our voices matter. As we grow prouder in our recovery, we grow louder in it too. The reason I recover out loud is to lead other women into recovery, to reach those suffering in silence. I want to help them so their words can take flight too.

Words matter. Especially when
we speak them out loud.

The Next Right Thing

Sometimes I get stuck. When I'm in the middle of a mess or a crisis, I often get or feel paralyzed and can't seem to make a decision or take action. It might not even be that big a problem; sometimes I'm just worn out from having made a million decisions already that day. One more thing to decide or do just feels like one too many. Not doing anything adds another layer of stress, of course, and that stress ramps up my anxiety.

The best way out of a mess or out of overwhelm is actually pretty straightforward. Just do the next right thing. Notice I said "thing," not "things." Pick one thing, one thing only. It can be a teeny-tiny thing that barely moves the needle on the issue, but at least it will move you from stuckness. Let your gut guide you as to what that thing should be. Keep it simple. Just taking that next right step will open the door to doing the next right thing after that. And so on.

A solution is made up of miniscule things.
Pick one and start.

• SEPTEMBER 18 •

Spiritual Awakenings

Early in my recovery from substance use, I heard that I would have a spiritual awakening if I worked the Steps in my Twelve Step program. I was all over that idea. Who wouldn't want a spiritual awakening? I got to work on those Steps almost immediately. I'm happy to report that I have had more than my fair share of awakenings over the course of my recovery, some because of "working the Steps" and some as a result of doing other recovery work. The awakenings have all been different, and most of them have presented subtly but with profound impact. One of the earliest awakenings came when I realized that I could be loved just for being me. Being accepted by other women in recovery was the catalyst for that awakening. Still is. Some years later, my spirit was blown open again when I realized that I could forgive people for not loving me the way that I deserved and needed to be loved. I think coming to know and believe this healed my heart more than anything. Those are just two examples of how my spirit has been awakened. I hope that there are more to come.

Our spirits awaken in recovery, providing us with a new way of being in the world.

• SEPTEMBER 19 •

The Difference Makers

When I look back over my life, I can recognize more than a few individuals who have made a difference in my life, and most of them probably don't even know it. Recovery invites us to take an inventory of our past, and as part of that work, I've spent some time thinking about those who acknowledged or supported me in some way, even if it was a small way. People like my sixth-grade teacher Mr. Walsh, who taught me all the required subjects and also convinced me that I was intelligent. I remember the first therapist I worked with who made me look at my own substance use after months of my talking only about my then-husband's addiction problem. That was a turning point in my life, to be sure. When I returned to university as a mature student, a professor listened to me as I poured my heart out about all the self-doubt I had about whether I could complete my degree because I had been so messed up for so long. She told me I could, and I did complete that degree—and two graduate degrees after it. I'm grateful for each of those difference makers. Who are yours?

You can be a difference maker for someone too.

Knowing When to Go Deeper

The thing about recovery is that we can be rolling along doing well in our lives, and then something will happen, or we will start to notice a new pattern, and it will become apparent that it's time to dig in and do more intensive self-development work. Thankfully, by this point in my life, I have learned to listen to my intuition and to trust myself enough to know when it's time to go back to the drawing board of my recovery. I'm a bit stubborn, so I might think I can handle whatever is crunchy in my life on my own for a spell, but then it becomes obvious that I can't. I might take a course or read a few books, thinking those things will get me into a better place, and those things might make a dent of a difference. Inevitably for me, I'll admit that I need more therapy. I will not be thrilled with this realization, and I might resist it for a while, but I'll feel more hopeful as soon as I set up an appointment with a therapist and start the process of going deeper into what's happening for me.

I do what I need to do to get at the core of my continued healing.

Making Amends

As Freya North once said, "It's not a person's mistakes which define them—it's the way they make amends." It's not just saying we are sorry about things that we may have done in the past, although that can be part of it. Some people may not want to hear from us ever again, and we need to honor that. When we do make verbal amends, we admit mistakes, but it isn't always about making right what was wrong. Sometimes making amends involves listening to others describe how what we did affected them. We can make indirect or direct amends. Once we offer them, we move on from our amends. Clearing up bad energy is important.

I don't believe in making direct amends if there is a chance that doing so might injure myself or others. Making amends is about making better or improving, amending our behaviors and our actions. It's not about repentance for me. It's about taking responsibility and changing my behavior. And sometimes it's even an opportunity to show others how much I've changed—that my amends show themselves in me.

Though we can't take back the past,
recovery gives us opportunities
to change the future.

• SEPTEMBER 22 •

Positive Language

Strengths-based, positive language matters, and what receives attention grows, so focusing on our weaknesses is not in our best interest. What if I had been invited to focus on my strengths throughout my life, rather than my defects? What if I were guided to ask what was right about me, good about me, about what I did well? We need to acknowledge our own inherent strengths. We need to focus on our own self-determination. A strengths-based approach, not a shame-based approach, will yield much better results. We all have potential. We all have strengths. We are all capable. We need to find and then use the language that lifts us up and release the words that we whisper to ourselves or speak aloud that tear us down.

What are some of your strengths? What do you know is right about you? Good about you? What do you do well? Can you be mindful about the words you use regularly to talk about yourself?

Remember to talk about your strengths,
especially when your weaknesses seem louder.

• SEPTEMBER 23 •

Feel Them to Heal Them

The thing about painful emotions is that you just can't reason with them. Before I started my recovery journey, most of my life was devoted to finding ways not to feel. Bless them always, but neither of my parents were into expressing "negative" feelings—not ours and not theirs. Messages like "Dry those tears" and "Oh, just never mind" and the popular-back-then admonition "I'll give you something to cry for" were ever-present in our home.

In early recovery, I spent a lot of time exploring my feelings intellectually but still trying to avoid experiencing them. That worked for a short while. Over time, I became willing to excavate the deep, dark, painful feelings that I had buried for so long. Working through those feelings meant a lot of tear-soaked days in therapy, crying so hard that every muscle in my face ached. Feeling hard feelings is exhausting, but not as exhausting as running from them. Bringing those dark emotions to the surface, feeling them, and then releasing them is an act of self-love.

Feeling and processing sadness
can make room for more happiness.

• SEPTEMBER 24 •

Going to the Water

I view my dear friend Elaine Alec, author of *Calling My Spirit Back*, as a sort of spiritual goddess, but really, she is one of the most down-to-earth women I know. A political advisor, women's advocate, and spiritual thought leader and teacher, Elaine is also an Indigenous woman in long-term recovery. She recovers out loud often and proudly. Her given name is *telxnitkw*, which means "standing by water." In her culture, a lot of women have names that are tied to the water, because a lot of their teachings are tied to the water. Elaine was taught by her elders that when she is having a hard time or facing a challenge, she needs to go to the water. I am in awe of Elaine's connection to wise women elders, and I honor her close connection to the water. Water is also a big part of my spiritual practice; I find a lot of my own answers at the ocean's edge. Getting to know Elaine has reminded me of the beauty of Indigenous wisdom and how applicable it is to recovery.

I am grateful for the women who generously share their cultural teachings; we have so much to learn from one another in recovery.

• SEPTEMBER 25 •

Who's on Your Team?

Since the beginning of my recovery journey, I've been surrounded by a team of people who believe in my ability to recover, who provide hope, support, and direction. The members of my team have changed over the years and decades, but most of the roles that people have played have remained the same. I have always had at least one wise *mentor*—someone with many more years of healing experience than me. At times this role has been filled by a sponsor from a Twelve Step program, other times a spiritual teacher from some other tradition. There have always been plenty of *peers* on the team, women who were or are at the same stage of recovery as I am. Many of these people have been by my side for over three decades, but I add new ones all the time. These are the women I hang with, whom I laugh and cry with regularly. Finally, in my view, no team would be complete without a few *professionals* here and there. I gratefully credit a long line of therapists, coaches, teachers, and medical professionals with enhancing my recovery journey.

My team members cheer me on and guide me in my recovery. Do you have a team? Are you on someone's team?

• SEPTEMBER 26 •

Everybody Needs Somebody

But do we? Do we really? Do we need somebody, or do we need somebodies? Is it too much pressure to have that one somebody who is our person? Our person to laugh with, cry with; our someone to believe in us, support us, teach us? Can one person meet all those needs? I say not. I am a person with a whole hell of a lot of somebodies in my life, and I wouldn't have it any other way.

People often remark that they don't know how I handle having so many recovering women in my life. To start with, I don't handle them. Nor do I collect them out of fear that I might need extras or that I might wear any one of them out. I just remain open to having a lot of wonderful, interesting women in my life, and they show up. I try to connect with as many of them as I can and form friendships with a great many. I also have a close inner circle of women who are my main somebodies, and I always have room for more of them too.

There's no such thing as too big a support system.

• SEPTEMBER 27 •

Being of Service

In the recovery circles that I devoted myself to for many years, there was a real emphasis on being of service. There still is. And while I do believe that those of us who are privileged enough to have found recovery need to pay things forward, I think that we need to do it in a balanced way. For the first period of my recovery, I volunteered to chair multiple meetings per week, sat on group committees, started an area service committee in my basement, and even held a position on a national board. Ironically, it was an entry in a daily meditation book that transformed how I thought about service. That entry, from the Narcotics Anonymous *Just for Today* book, basically suggested that our families don't benefit from our recovery if we are never home to share it with them, that rushing out to meetings every night of the week might still feel like abandonment to them. Practicing the principles of recovery in all our affairs means paying attention to the people at home, perhaps even first and foremost, when being of service. Showing up for ourselves in recovery and helping others in or seeking recovery is important, but recovery matters at home too. Full stop.

We recover for ourselves but also for those we love. Being of service at home shows our loved ones that they matter.

• SEPTEMBER 28 •

Recovery Is a Practice

I'm passionate about reminding people that recovery is something that we get to design for ourselves, and that includes defining how and at what pace it unfolds. Recovery can only be fairly and properly defined by the individual seeking or living in it. The concept of having a recovery *practice* lends itself well to such ideas. When it comes to *my* recovery, what my recovery practice is made up of, and for what purpose or outcome, is up to *me*. Your practice of recovery is up to *you*. Your loved one in, or seeking, recovery will have to determine their recovery practice and will need your support in that practice and how it might evolve over time.

The concept of recovery as a practice works particularly well for women who have a history of feeling disempowered in their lives and/or their recovery. This is especially true for women who have been impacted by abuse, systemic racism, and other traumas. The more opportunities we each have to exercise agency and choice in defining both the parameters and the patchwork pieces of our recovery, the better.

We design our own practice for recovery, and then we commit to following it imperfectly.

• SEPTEMBER 29 •

Recovery Is Not a Race

When I chose recovery, I felt like I was so behind in my life that I had to make time up quickly. I had to straighten out, smarten up, and get a move on. Or so I thought. My pace in early recovery can best be described as frantic. I barreled through the Twelve Steps in the first couple of years, went to work to get off welfare and take care of my daughters, and barely had my feet on the ground before I dove into intensive therapy and went back to school. I stayed in school for thirteen years. I got so used to *busy* that I turned into a workaholic.

If you are early in recovery, even if your life feels like a train wreck (mine was), I'd like to give you some advice that I wish I had taken myself (more than a few people gave it to me). Work hard at your recovery, get yourself together, and sort out your life. But don't try to fix everything at once. Tend to the obvious things first; you know what they are. Then be sure to tackle the non-urgent things mindfully. You will be surprised how gentle change can be when you set your own parameters.

Recovery is not a race; it's a practice and a lifestyle, and we can embrace it gently.

Humility

A few years ago, a debate emerged in the women's recovery community about the concept of humility. A friend of mine, someone I love and respect, suggested that when it comes to women's recovery, we should do away with the concept of humility entirely. A great many women I know agreed. I understand the impulse, if we think about humility in terms of women being modest or unassuming, lacking pride, or being submissive. However, humility does not conjure up strong feelings of disempowerment for me. Rather, in my life, having humility is all about acknowledging that I am still learning, that I don't have all the answers, whether related to recovery or any other thing. Admitting that I still have things to learn has always been a source of empowerment for me and an impetus for my growth. But that's just me.

Humbly asking for more information and guidance can be a precursor to growth.

OCTOBER

Finding Stillness

Stillness can be defined as the absence of movement or sound. It's about solitude, silence, tranquility. It's about presence. Stillness can be elusive. Stillness doesn't even necessarily mean still. I know that things can still shift and move even in stillness. That stillness is a prerequisite to understanding and insights, both requiring movement in our minds.

I love the phrase *inner quietude.* When I'm in inner quietude, I can hear the voice within my inner secrets. I can ask questions in the stillness and hear the answers, or feel them. Pausing external noise and activity leads me most easily to stillness. I pause as often as I can to experience stillness throughout my day. I find it in my morning practice; I create it at least once more during the day. I love to find stillness in nature, especially at the beach. I sit in stillness and feel the sun and the wind or the drizzle of a light rain. Tranquility is my friend. Clarity is the outcome. Tranquility is my friend. Clarity is the outcome.

Stillness can move so much,
especially our hearts and minds.

• OCTOBER 2 •

Imaginary Relationships

My friend Holly Whitaker wrote something recently about going to visit, possibly for the last time, a person she had imagined herself to be in a relationship with. It was such a powerful admission—and one that struck a deep chord in me. During a long period of love addiction in my early years, I concocted an imaginary relationship with a person who I now know had feelings for me but not a desire to be with me, despite my having given birth to his beautiful daughter. He might have wanted her, but he didn't want me. Still, I imagined us as a family for the first two years of her life, although he was in our physical presence only once during that time. Letters and phone calls between us fed my fantasy in one moment, but that fantasy would come crashing down in the next. When I gave up this imaginary relationship, I fell deep into my addiction for a while, got into another relationship that was very real and very bad, and had another beautiful baby girl. It was only in recovery that I finally found a person to love me in real life, as I was and as I am. Imaginary relationships are painful, and I'm glad mine are behind me.

When love is for real, you will know it.

• OCTOBER 3 •

Addressing Our Shadows

No matter how far you think you have fallen at times in your life, you are not an evil person, not even if you believe that some of the things you did in your past are unforgivable. When I first began addressing my dark times as part of my healing journey, I unearthed a list of troubling things that I had done during my active addiction, things that I wanted to stay buried. I didn't think I could ever deal with—or let go of—most of those things. But I have.

If you think there is value in it, you can visit your darkness and the dark times in your life, but you don't have to live there anymore. You can learn what you need to from those times by being in reflection on your own, in conversation with other people in recovery, or in therapy. Spiritual teacher Iyanla Vanzant says that it is our willingness to look at our darkness that empowers us to change. When you look at your darkness, or your shadows, do it with compassion, not judgment, and with self-love, not self-reproach.

We have all had dark periods in our past;
we can shine light on them and release them.

• OCTOBER 4 •

Our Imperfect Families of Origin

I can still suffer a little bit around things having to do with my family of origin, but I've gotten so much better at just accepting and loving members of that family as they are. I accept that I won't in this lifetime have the relationship with my older brothers that I once wished for, but I believe that they love me in their own way. My father and I found a beautiful closeness as he entered the final season of his life, and that is good enough for me. Because of my recovery, I was able to form a very close relationship with my mother in the years before she passed away, which was beautiful but made losing her so hard. After five years of estrangement, I now have a loving relationship with my sister, who also has years in recovery. Watching her heal and grow has meant the world to me. Family-of-origin things are hard. We often avoid these issues because they are so complicated and seemingly insurmountable. And some of them are. Some things in our families can't be resolved. But a few of them can.

The most rewarding growth is never easy.

Introvert or Extrovert?

I used to think that everyone had to be categorized as either introvert or extrovert, and I've always struggled to know which of the two applies to me. Younger me identified as an extrovert, meaning that I drew my energy from people, places, and things outside of myself. But also, I couldn't stand myself, so I didn't look to myself for much of anything. After some time in recovery, I thought I had transformed into an introvert, someone who turns inward and draws more energy from being alone. I really, really like time alone. And I trust and look to myself for all kinds of things now.

As it turns out, I didn't have to pick one or the other personality trait, because I am and have always been an ambivert, someone who falls in the middle of the introvert/extrovert continuum and has a blend of traits from both. It makes sense for me to know that I haven't changed from one to another; I've always been both. My answer to the question "Would you rather be around people or have time alone?" is very easily "It depends." How do you answer that question? Whatever you are, I hope you find your balance.

Being in the "middle" of a personality spectrum feels like balance to me.

• OCTOBER 6 •

Childhood Dreams

When I was a little girl, I aspired to be an actress. I loved to play make-believe with cousins and friends, years after others my age had moved on to presumably more mature activities. From the age of five, I was allowed to stay up late with my mom to watch the Academy Awards, and I spent hours in front of the mirror practicing my acceptance speech. I finally got the opportunity to take the stage in middle school, when our fifth-grade class put on *Anne of Green Gables.* I wanted to play Anne, of course, and was devastated when I was asked to play her foster mother, Marilla, instead. As I held back tears of disappointment, my teacher took me aside and whispered to me, "Oh my dear, any little girl can play Anne. It takes a real actress to play Marilla." I went on to take acting lessons and even performed in one professional play before I gave up my dream for drugs. I've never returned to that dream, but I still might someday. I'm sure there's some community theater that's just the right place for me.

Downsized dreams can come true too.

• OCTOBER 7 •

What's Your Thing?

While it might seem overwhelming to admit we all have a *thing* (or two) to recover from, the principle that "we are all recovering from something" is intended to be hopeful, not depressing. Admitting that we each have something to address in our lives is one of the best ways to reduce stigma, because when everyone admits to having a *thing*, then it's no big deal to have a thing. There might be a tendency for some of us to think that our thing is not as bad or as serious as somebody else's thing, but that's not useful and defeats the purpose, so please don't be doing that.

The "Everyone has something" principle is as helpful as it is hopeful because when some of us share the same things, we can also share our strategies and solutions for recovering from them. Sharing information and our experience is practical and resourceful. It also makes things beautifully inclusive for women looking for a supportive community when they can access so many different solutions.

Bring all your things with you into recovery.
No shame. No judgment.

• OCTOBER 8 •

Bearing Unbearable Loss

If you have been through something tragic and unbearable in your life, I am so sorry. I hope that you haven't, but if you have, I honor you and your grief and want to acknowledge you for still being here. Some of the people I know who now live on this side of tragedy have told me that they didn't believe they could live through it. I'm so glad they did. They told me that the only way they got through their own unbearable grief was to breathe through it. Others have shared how their loss opened their heart and their mind to a new life purpose. Some work as advocates in areas related to their loss; the work they do honors the loved ones they lost.

Everyone who has survived a personal tragedy of great magnitude can attest to the transformational nature of unbearable grief and to the fact that love is strengthened—not lost—in loss. Author and inspirational speaker Elizabeth Gilbert got it exactly right when she said, "It's an honor to be in grief. It's an honor to feel that much, to have loved that much."

Somehow, sometimes, we do
survive the unbearable.

• OCTOBER 9 •

What You Deserve

At many points along our recovery journey, we will seek and secure professional help. When we do, we need to be sure that the people we engage welcome us as full partners in our own care. They need to respect our sexuality, gender identity, and race as well as understand our values, experiences, and perspectives regarding what we need. They need to recognize the impacts that stress and trauma have had on our health and be able to communicate empathetically and effectively with us so that we can build trust and mutual understanding. They need to listen to us as we explore and put together our recovery patchwork; they don't have the right to dissuade us from following particular pathways. We always deserve to be the final decision makers on our recovery plans. Importantly, if or when we have a setback in our recovery, we deserve professionals' support, not their judgment. Are you receiving the support that you deserve?

I define the sort of professional support
that I will receive, when I determine
that I need it.

• OCTOBER 10 •

Words Are Powerful

Words matter in recovery, especially in addiction recovery. For example, the language that we use when we talk about people who experience substance use issues can either build them up or tear them down. To stay on the "building up" side of things, we use people-first language that focuses on the person, not the substance use. To that end, we refer to a person with a substance use disorder exactly in that way, rather than as an addict or alcoholic. But how people choose to refer to *themselves* is completely up to them. People in Twelve Step recovery, for example, are often proud to call themselves addicts or alcoholics. Those words are powerful for them, and they claim those identities gratefully. We need to respect that.

I choose the language and the labels that work for my recovery, and you can do the same.

• OCTOBER 11 •

A Work in Progress

Hello, you. Yes, you. Reading this book. Why are you so hard on yourself these days? Have you celebrated where you are on your journey lately, even if you aren't exactly where you want to be? Have you given yourself credit just for being here, for being willing, even just for having the awareness that you have some work to do? Having awareness is a big deal; don't underestimate its power. You are a work in progress, and you may have a ways to go to reach your goals and live your dreams, but the key word is *progress.* Every day that you think about wanting to live a different version of your life is a good day. Every day that you get up and get moving is a day to celebrate your strength and fortitude. Things haven't always been easy, have they? Maybe even yesterday was hard. Being a work in progress, the other key word in that phrase is *work.* Keep working. You are so much further along than you give yourself credit for.

The masterpiece that is our life is not complete.
We keep moving forward with hope.

Three Goddesses Are Better Than One

By my second year in recovery, I realized that I needed to develop a relationship with a higher power that wasn't as small as a rock or as expansive as the entire universe. By no small coincidence, I was led to the book *Goddesses in Everywoman* by Jean Shinoda Bolen as part of a women's studies course that I was taking. I thought I would choose the goddess who most resonated with me, but I soon determined that a goddess *trifecta* would be more to my liking. So I chose three goddesses to guide me in my life and in my recovery. I called upon Athena, goddess of wisdom and logic, for all things related to being a mature student in university. Artemis was there to spur on my independent feminine spirit as I railed against the patriarchy (did I mention I was a women's studies major?). And pulling all that intense intellectual and activist energy together was Hestia, goddess of inner centeredness. Those three gals helped me out a lot in early recovery, and I still call upon them occasionally.

Goddesses make great higher powers.

Saying Sorry Counts

One day you will realize or remember that something you once said or did to another human being caused that person harm and pain. You will be ashamed and sorry, and you will wish that you could take it back. You cannot. But you can do something to address what happened, something that can help you and that person too. In Twelve Step recovery this is called "making amends." *To amend* means to change, so changing your behavior and never doing that hurtful thing again is a lot more meaningful than just saying you are sorry. But apologies count too. You can go to the person or maybe write to that person and sincerely tell them how sorry you are for your words, actions, or inaction, whatever the case may be. You can say, "I am so sorry, and I want you to know that, and I want you to know that I have changed."

Here's the thing: that person may or may not be open to hearing your apology, and even if they do, they may not be ready or willing to forgive you. That's okay, and you will just need to let that be. Still, you will feel a great burden lift just for having made the effort.

We can't change the past, but we can
soften the pain of some of it.

The Old-Timers

When I was little, there was rarely a day that went by when I didn't hear the phrase "Respect your elders." I generally heeded the warning because it was delivered as more of a threat than a suggestion. In any case, the point was made repeatedly, and I did, indeed, learn how to respect my elders. When I got to recovery, there was some similarly clear messaging that the wonderful elder statesmen and stateswomen in the Twelve Step program that saved my life were to be respected. And for good reason. The women (sorry, guys, it's just not usually about you with me) who came before me in recovery were initially my idols, then they became my mentors, and eventually many became my friends. Today, I am blessed to have in my recovery life and in my recovery work women whom I look up to and continue to learn from. I am very grateful for one such old-timer (that's what people in long-term recovery are called) who has guided my daughter and me as we embarked on a new level of service, starting a nonprofit focused on women's recovery. As with all of the old-timers I have known, her wisdom was hard-won. Her respect has been easily earned.

I remember with love and respect
the women who came before me
or alongside me in recovery.

• OCTOBER 15 •

Embracing All of Who We Are

I continue to learn a lot about recovery from my sweet friend Lisa, an amazing woman in recovery from codependency. Lisa borrows a definition of *codependency* from another brilliant friend of ours—Nikki Myers—who says that codependency is "the disease of looking elsewhere." How simple but profound is that definition? In her writing and in recovery gatherings, Lisa shares about the magic of being able to transform previously maladaptive coping behaviors into gifts that now enhance her life and her recovery. For example, with a little radical self-love and some honest conversations with herself, her hypervigilance slowly transformed into deep empathic abilities and the gift of being able to read energy. Perfectionism shifted to the ability to pay greater attention to detail. A desire to please others turned into a passion for being of service and loving herself, radically. An obsession with maintaining a positive outlook at all costs morphed into a desire to hold space for myriad feelings all at once, from joy to grief. Talk about turning lead into gold—this woman is nailing recovery.

Here's to embracing the dark and the light parts of ourselves and becoming more authentic, whole, and integrated human beings.

• OCTOBER 16 •

Rest First

What do you think about when you hear the word *rest*? I almost always think of rest as something that is only done between other things, and for most of my life, I always gave those other things more attention than any rest periods between. Lately I've been practicing something quite different: I am trying to prioritize rest over activity, to rest first and do later. Some days I fail miserably at it, but I shall persevere because I see the benefits when I succeed at it. Resting first means easing into my day, mindfully and gently. It means saying no to requests for my time so that I can take regular pauses throughout each day. It means being purposefully unproductive by doing things like reading my novel in the middle of the afternoon between work commitments. Resting first means looking at my Day-Timer at the beginning of each month and scheduling days off—and then keeping them free. As a recovering workaholic, I've learned that figuring out my rest schedule is more important than my work schedule. I still have a lot to learn, but I'm on my way.

Prioritizing rest above all the other things may not feel natural, but it sure does feel good.

Recognizing and Challenging Our Prejudices

We all have attitudes and judgments that we hold against people or groups, and we can only begin to let go of those prejudices if we admit that. When I was in university, one of my professors had a profound impact on me when she said to us, "Don't ask yourself *if* you are racist; ask yourself *how* you are racist." We all have strong inclinations to answer no when asked if we are racist, but when we ask ourselves *how* instead, that can be an invitation for self-reflection. I find that the best starting point for me is to examine my privilege as a white, middle-class, educated professional woman. From within this sphere of privilege, I know that I make assumptions about other individuals or groups of people regardless of their race, ethnicity, political affiliation, and so on. Unconsciously or not, I am sure I bring those judgments out into the world. I can do better when I know better. Do you ask yourself the hard "how" questions, or do you take the easy "if" way out?

None of us are without prejudices; we need to admit that to change and grow. It's one of the ways we can keep our side of the street clean in recovery.

• OCTOBER 18 •

Quieting the Voices

We are all recovering from something, but as much as anything—I believe—most of us are recovering from living with the voice or voices in our head that invite feelings of low self-esteem, self-doubt, and even self-hatred. I'm talking about the voices that whisper to us throughout our lives that we aren't enough—or aren't worthy of being here. For many, those voices are the voices that we heard in our childhood, from our parents or other important people in our lives. Not all of them intended to do harm with the things they said, but that doesn't mean harm wasn't done. Other voices are related to people who played to our insecurities, or worse, abused us. At some points in my life, those damaging voices hollered. Today they are much quieter, but they are still there, trying to sabotage me once in a while. The difference is that I've learned how to listen for them, acknowledge them, and tell them to shut the hell up.

If we listen really carefully, we hear the things that build us up, not tear us down.

Change

Change takes courage, especially when it comes at the end of a long period of wishing, wanting, and hoping for change—but not being ready to do what it takes to make change a reality. I've made some rather monumental changes in my life, and I am willing to bet you have too. Every change I have made started with a decision I made without fully understanding what change would look like. It's like author and motivational speaker Mel Robbins says: sometimes we are "one decision away from a completely different life."

Making big changes in our life also takes time and practice, especially when the change is about stopping a behavior. If you have made the decision to stop doing something, just keep practicing and trying. Focus on how you feel when you *do* succeed at stopping, and then celebrate your success. On those days or at those times when you are not able to change something, forgive yourself and try again. You will be inclined to feel bad about yourself, to start beating yourself up. Change that behavior too.

We need courage to change because
change is hard, but it's not impossible.

• OCTOBER 20 •

Loving Ourselves Sober

A few years ago, I was honored to write the foreword for a lovely book entitled *Love Yourself Sober*, written by two of my equally lovely British friends, Kate Baily and Mandy Manners. In addition to being an optimistic and helpful handbook for finding and maintaining sobriety (from alcohol), Kate and Mandy's book sets out to crush the myth that, as the Cambridge English Dictionary purports, to be sober is "to become calmer and more serious." These two Brits call bullshit on that outlook and invite newly sober women to "bring on the sparkle." They invite us to feel the awesomeness of a sober life and to love it. I subscribe to their approach. From the moment I met him thirty years ago, my own partner (in life and in recovery) has also preached the doctrine that if you aren't having at least some fun in recovery, you need to switch things up. Recovery is to be celebrated, regardless of what we are recovering from. There's a lot of hard work to recovery, to staying sober or healing other maladaptive coping mechanisms. Looking for the light and the laughter in recovery is a necessity.

We can love ourselves into and through our recovery; we need to try to have fun throughout all of it.

• OCTOBER 21 •

Collaboration over Competition

When I started out talking about women's recovery in cyberspace, there weren't a whole heck of a lot of us doing it. In fact, in the North American context, the number of widely read blogs and related platforms would have numbered less than a dozen at the end of the first decade of the twenty-first century. The landscape has transformed in recent years. The number of women's recovery platforms—most with a focus on alcohol, but also recovery platforms more broadly—has exploded and continues to grow. This is a very good thing. We need a lot of choices because we all need something different. Everyone should be encouraged to design and deliver resources that are meaningful to them and the women they hope to reach. But here's the most important piece: we need to support one another in all our efforts. We need to collaborate and share with one another, and we need to refer out to one another. One of the She Recovers Intentions & Guiding Principles reads, "Connection is our sole (soul) purpose. We're stronger together." Do you agree?

There is strength in numbers, and there is
more than enough need to go around
for all to make an impact.

More about Perfectionism

One of my favorite authors, Anne Wilson Schaef, once wrote, "Perfectionism is self-abuse of the highest order." How powerful is that statement? Children who experience emotional neglect (well, okay, I'm talking specifically about me here) think that if we can just be perfect in all the things that we do, our parents will love and adore us. We (okay, I) strive for perfection throughout childhood and into adulthood. Some of us (me again) keep beating ourselves up with perfectionism, but others of us (pick me for this one) get to a point where we just say, "Screw it, I'm never going to be perfect enough for them. I might as well blow up my life." Please note, what precedes is my made-up psychological model; my PhD is in health care policy, so I'm not really qualified to develop social and psychological theories. The point is, I have been a person who abused myself through perfectionism. I took a break from it to become addicted to drugs for a decade but picked it up again as part of my workaholism. I try hard not to hurt myself with perfectionism anymore.

Perfectionism hurts ourselves the most;
no amount of perfect is worth the pain.

Sensitivity as a Superpower

How many of us in recovery have been called "too sensitive"? I'm thinking there are more than a few of us. I certainly grew up hearing the "Don't be so sensitive" refrain from the adults around me. Crying was taboo, and I wasn't encouraged to talk about my hurt feelings. As a mother and grandmother, I can almost empathize with the adults who reacted to my emotional sensitivity as they did. I don't like to see the little ones I love cry, because it breaks my heart. But we know better today (I hope) than to shut down our loved ones' feelings. When I see my daughters lean into their sensitive feelings (one of them leans more easily than the other), it makes me think I did something right. Elizabeth Bishop, author of *Conscious Service: Ten Ways to Reclaim Your Calling, Move beyond Burnout, and Make a Difference without Sacrificing Yourself*, tells us that our sensitivity is our *superpower*, in our work and in our lives. I love her outlook, which includes an understanding that when we connect with our emotional sensitivity, we are less likely to abandon ourselves. She encourages us to listen to our sensitivity when it is present. I can do that. Can you?

We are sensitive souls, we women in recovery.
Let's be gentle with ourselves and one another.

• OCTOBER 24 •

Scarcity Mindset

I have had to do a lot of work in my recovery—well, okay, I still have to work at it—to not operate from a scarcity mindset. I'm getting better at it, but in the past, I was often driven by fear that there was never going to be enough of what I needed: love, food (sometimes), money, and—especially relevant for someone who struggles with overworking—time.

When I'm in a scarcity mindset, it's hard to think about anything else other than the lack that I am obsessed with. Fortunately, there are practices that help me get out of that mindset. I can even stay out of a scarcity mindset if I practice these things regularly. The first practice is for me to meditate on all that I have and the deep knowing that I will always be taken care of. The second practice is keeping a running written gratitude list. The third is to surround myself with and engage with people who operate from an abundance mindset and can keep me centered in remembering that I will always have enough. Or more.

I am blessed with the gifts of time,
nourishment, and emotional support.
I work hard to remember this.

• OCTOBER 25 •

Just Winging It over Here

Despite having a lot of personal experience with recovery, and even though my career is focused on researching and writing about women, mental health, and addiction, I never want to be thought of as someone who has all the answers. Or even a lot of the answers. I have a lot of ideas and opinions and thoughts about women in recovery and a solid evidence and knowledge base, but also, I often feel like I'm just winging it when I talk or write about what works in women's recovery. I say that not because I don't value my own expertise, but because my expertise is based largely on my lived and living experience, as well as what I observe and have observed in other women who are in recovery. You also have expertise, and I hope that you know and believe that. You are very much an expert in your own recovery. Perhaps you feel like I do, that living our lives in recovery is a little bit of knowledge coupled with a whole bunch of experimentation. I'm glad we are in this together and can learn from one another.

Women's recovery is a field of its own,
and I love that we get to play
in that field together.

In the End

It is often said, "In the end, only three things matter: how much you loved, how gently you lived, and how gracefully you let go of things not meant for you." I am nowhere near ready for anything to end, but I feel like I am rocking the whole "things that matter" goal. I have loved intensely and have plenty of time and room to love more. I learned how to let go a few years into my recovery; it wasn't particularly graceful in the beginning, but I got better at it and mostly master it these days. Today, one of my own personal growth goals is to bring more gentleness into my days and to be more tender toward myself, others, and the world. I know that I still have a few edges that could use softening; being gentle doesn't always come easily. Fortunately for me, there's another saying that goes, "Everything will be okay in the end. If it's not okay, it's not the end." Thanks for that one, John Lennon.

I know that one day, when this all ends,
I will have lived a life that matters.

• OCTOBER 27 •

Device Addiction

Although I am loath to admit it, I sometimes worry that I am addicted to my smartphone. These days, our phones can report back to us on how much time we are spending on them, and from what I hear from people in my life, most of us are regularly surprised by how much time that is. I'm not a person who is able to be abstinent from my phone, but I try to practice moderation. I make up phone rules for myself, and I do my best to follow them. For instance, I try not to take my phone into my bedroom at night unless I need to set an alarm (I rarely need to set an alarm). I have removed all social media apps on my phone, which has made the biggest difference. I don't take my phone to the park when I go with my grandchildren, and I leave it in the car when I'm hanging out at the beach. Just these few things keep me more regulated with my phone behavior. What is your relationship with your phone?

Putting down my phone allows me
to practice presence with the people
I love, including myself.

Dads and Daughters

In 1987, I called my parents to tell them that I was going to treatment to deal with my substance use problem. They knew that I had some struggles in that area but had never confronted me directly about it. We didn't have the language to have such conversations back then. My mom was clearly upset by my call, but I heard a hint of hopefulness in her voice too. She handed my dad the phone. I will never for as long as I live forget what he said to me, mostly because he hadn't really said a whole lot to me up until that point in my life. To his credit, he knew how to find words when I most needed them. He told me that I was doing the right thing and that there was no shame in getting help for a problem. And then, just before he handed the phone back to my mother, he said, "You have always had balls, and I know you can beat this thing." His words have stuck with me ever since, and I remind myself of them whenever I am afraid to do something that I know I have to do.

People can surprise us,
exactly when we need them to.

The Costs of Being Right

For the longest time in my life (before recovery), I needed to be right. I worked hard and campaigned to be right. Like so many things in my life before recovery, it was always about control—trying to control other people, what they thought, or how they thought about me. It was exhausting, for me and for anyone around me. My close friend Jean McCarthy, host of the popular sobriety podcast *The Bubble Hour* and author of a series of helpful books on sobriety, knows what I'm talking about, as evidenced by one of her *UnPickled* blog posts that I read recently. In it, Jean recounts how, one day, after she had expended considerable effort trying to convince her husband of something, her eleven-year-old son, who had been watching and listening, looked at his mom and simply said, "You, like, really enjoy being *right*." That really impacted Jean. As she reflected, she realized that she would have been defensive and wounded if an adult had said that to her, but she found herself receptive to the honest observation coming from her own child. Jean and I are both more okay these days with not being right.

It's better to invest our energy in letting go of control than in being right. When we release the need to be right, we learn a lot.

If I Had a Choice

I nearly lost my life four times to addiction and once to stage III colon cancer. Today, if I were given the choice between having cancer again or falling back into active addiction, I'd be inclined to choose cancer. Not that cancer wasn't hard; it was. I was within an hour of my death when emergency surgery saved my life, and a year of intensive chemotherapy saved it again. My odds of surviving five years weren't great, but I have accomplished that more than threefold. So, while it sounds somewhat drastic, I think that the odds of me surviving active drug addiction again would be lower than my cancer odds. When I use substances addictively, I self-destruct. My life becomes one of confusion, pain, and chaos, completely unpredictable. A cancer diagnosis, even a terminal one, would allow me some predictability. I'd gratefully spend whatever time given me in gratitude, surrounded by loving friends and family and doing the things I love to do most. Clearly, I'm never going to be given two such morbid choices, but I feel good knowing where I'd probably stand.

I would choose presence in my life
over escaping it, time and time again.

Partnerships in Recovery

Before meeting my life partner, my history with romantic partners was rather nightmarish. My "picker" was broken, which meant my heart usually was too. Several relationships were outright abusive but felt normal to me, as I was so abusive to myself. A few years into my recovery, I realized that I was worth a whole lot more than I'd been settling for previously. I made a list of what I wanted in a partner, and I stuck to it. I found him at a Twelve Step convention, and we got to know each other as friends for six months before things got romantic. That had never happened before, and I highly recommend it. I don't take for granted how fortunate I am to have someone who does life with me, takes absolute care of me, and reminds me that I don't have to do everything by myself. We aren't perfect. We drive each other crazy at times. When things get scratchy between us, as they inevitably do, we each have a recovery practice and peers to help us sort ourselves out. We are good together, but we also benefit from time apart. We work. I'm grateful that I have learned how to let someone love me. Have you learned how to do that too?

Hearts open to healthy love in recovery.

NOVEMBER

Altars

Since the early days of my recovery, I've always had an altar of sorts set up on the dresser in my bedroom, or on the top of a bookshelf in my office. The artifacts on my altars are sentimental and meaningful, and most of them reach back into the past. My current altar hosts a tall ceramic goddess figure, a glass candle of the Virgin Mary, a large amethyst crystal and a small rose quartz one, a picture of my late mom, a rosary, a rollerball bottle of frankincense, and my favorite tarot deck. My altar rituals are simple. I light the candle when the world feels upside down or in honor of loved ones who have passed or who are unwell or struggling, and I pull from my tarot deck most mornings. I take a moment every so often to anoint my wrists with frankincense and inhale the scent slowly and purposefully. For me, an altar is an intentional space to honor life and love, a visual reminder to breathe and be grateful. My altar is also a tradition of sorts, as I've heard it said that the tops of our mothers' and grandmothers' dressers were types of altars too.

My altar is a sacred space that both represents and influences my personal energy.

• NOVEMBER 2 •

The Seasons of Grief

Grief changes like the seasons, and it comes around just as surely. In the aftermath of loss, we feel numb, in shock, unable to process thoughts or complete tasks. Emotional and physical paralysis may be the norm. When we do start easing back into our life, our movements can feel robotic and programmed; even so, it feels like progress. We might not be feeling anything emotionally, but moving our body and pretending that things are normal occasionally can feel scary, like we are dismissing our grief and the thing or person we are grieving. That feels like betrayal to us. Timelines vary, but eventually we find ourselves feeling a little lighter, and after a while, lighter still. It might take a long time before we smile or laugh again, but one day we will. It's important to know that we can be plunged back into fulsome grief at any time, and after a few rounds, a few seasons of the ups and downs, we will find our footing in our new normal. Life after whatever or whomever we lost will be forever different, but it's still our life, and we will find a way to live it.

Grief changes, ebbs, and flows.
But it's always there.

Time Does Not Heal All Wounds

We tell one another that time heals all wounds, because we want to believe that the pain we experience will go away, especially when we are right in the thick of it. But we are fooling ourselves if we think that our wounds will heal completely, as the saying suggests. They won't. And life still goes on. I once believed that I just needed time to heal the things that broke me, but decades later I've learned the truth. The pain lessens, thankfully. I figure out a way to function and find joy and even forget, for periods of time, the pain or the trauma that cut me to my core. But the wound is always there and can sometimes feel as fresh as if it just happened. Having regular reprieve from the wounds is a gift, but I also must remember and process them purposefully, sometimes. I think that psychotherapist Shadeen Francis got it right when she said, "Time doesn't heal wounds. Healing heals wounds."

With space and time, I learn how to live
with my wounds and accept that
they are a part of me.

• NOVEMBER 4 •

Forgiving Ourselves

I love the idea that when we know better, we do better. In early recovery, I found it impossibly hard to forgive myself for some of the things that I had done during my period of active addiction. But hating myself for those things took too high a toll, and I had to find a way to let go and move on. Two things helped me with self-forgiveness. The first was believing the recovering people around me who warned me that staying in shame and self-hatred would hinder—and possibly even destroy—my recovery process. That felt true to me. The second thing was embracing the idea that I heard from others (also in recovery) that when we know better, we do better. As the great Maya Angelou said, "Forgive yourself for not knowing what you didn't know before you learned it." How liberating is that?

Forgiving ourselves is one sure way to practice radical self-compassion. Try it?

An Ode to the Aunts

I grew up in a large, extended family where everybody knew that "the aunts" were in charge. The great-aunts, the regular aunts, and the women we called "aunt" who were just longtime family friends. I loved them all, even the ones I was slightly afraid of. They were mostly all nurturing, and each one focused on feeding us first, bossing us around second. They came in all sizes and personalities. Some were gentle and soft-spoken; a few others could drink and swear like sailors. Some were addicted, before me. There were family tragedies and big family wars, and it was hard sometimes to keep track of who wasn't speaking to whom. Still, nobody died who wasn't mourned by all. When my mom passed away, every aunt still living circled and held my sister and me. We're running out of aunts these days, and every loss hurts. I'm grateful for those who have passed and the few who remain. I'm grateful to come from an incredible line of fabulous women.

May I always remember the strength
and the love of the many women
I have called aunt.

• NOVEMBER 6 •

Our Internal Validation Voices

My friend Arlina Allen is the host of the *One Day At A Time Recovery Podcast*, a recovery coach, and a force in the women's recovery movement. Something she wrote recently really struck a chord in me. In her "How I Healed My Inner Validation Junkie" entry on the She Recovers blog, Arlina asked herself: What if all the validation and approval she ever wanted was already inside of her? And what if there are a bunch of different versions of her, all approving of her and validating her all the time? Whoah! What if that is true for all of us?

As Arlina ponders, what if every version of our internal self is crying out that we are enough, and uniquely amazing? What if we simply let that internal, validating voice be enough? Is there any reason we can't? We are in charge of our own thoughts; I say we decide what those thoughts will be. Let's let go of our need for external validation and practice validating ourselves. It can't hurt, right?

In an ideal world, we would be born
fully validated. Since that didn't happen,
let's validate ourselves.

• NOVEMBER 7 •

I Am Who I Am

Many years ago, a famous quote from Eleanor Roosevelt, former First Lady of the United States, caught my attention. She wrote, "Somehow we learn who we really are and then live with that decision." That reads to me as a two-step process, but not a process that has a hard stop at either end of it.

My recovery has been all about learning who I really am. What I like, what I believe, where and how I like to spend my time, with whom and doing what. I'm not done with this process of coming to know myself, and I'm not sure I ever will be. I know I am getting closer, but I am not quite there yet, Eleanor.

As I grow personally, and especially as I age, I continue to evolve and change. Sometimes I move in the wrong direction and need to course-correct. Regardless of who I think I am in any given moment, I have no difficulty living with who I have decided I am. I know that, ultimately, I am a good human. I am doing my best to live my full and imperfect life.

I'm okay with who I am, and I decide
every day how I am going to show up
as that person in the world.

• NOVEMBER 8 •

Fear of Time Running Out

The lovely thing about being in recovery is that I make good use of my time—much better use than when I was in active addiction, for sure. My biggest fear when I first found recovery was that I wouldn't have enough time to figure out what I was supposed to be doing with my life, let alone do it. I felt like I was so very behind, that I had lost a decade-plus to addiction, and I knew I could never get it back. I don't live (too much) in fear of time running out anymore. I mean, I *think* I don't. I do know that my length of time here on earth isn't promised. I had cancer. My mom died quite young. Hard to say how long I'll be hanging around. And still. My fear today is not so much about running out of time as it is about simply *wasting* the time left to me on things that really don't matter. Because I do waste time on things that don't matter. I really want to change that. I'm trying. Progress, not perfection.

Every minute matters; I try to
make the most of each one.

Dreams Do Come True

In *It Works, How and Why*, one of the program texts for the Twelve Step program Narcotics Anonymous, there is a lovely passage that reads, "We ask ourselves when we stopped believing in ourselves and when we stopped believing in anything outside ourselves. Through this process, our lost dreams may reawaken." In 2011, as I focused on healing from a bottom I hit with workaholism, I felt a long-lost dream reawaken. That dream was to become a writer. As I recovered, I started to blog about recovery, and I began to believe in myself and my abilities again. I also started to believe that external factors could align to support me in my dreams. The stars did align, and after a short period of time I found myself writing for a living—from home or from anywhere I wanted. That was another dream I had—to be mobile in my work and, importantly, to have a job where I don't have to wear a bra all day. This is my life today. My deepest dreams have come true.

Don't stop believing in your dreams,
or in the power of yourself and the
universe to realize them.

• NOVEMBER 10 •

Don't Give Up

There is an old Japanese proverb that goes, "Fall seven times, stand up eight." This is a good concept to grasp for those of us in recovery. Recovery takes commitment, it's not easy, and it very rarely unfolds in a straight line. Most people in recovery, regardless of what they are recovering from, experience setbacks. Actress Mackenzie Phillips, a friend and beloved figure in the She Recovers community, writes about the nonlinear nature of her own recovery from trauma and a near-fatal substance use disorder in her book *Hopeful Healing: Essays on Managing Recovery and Surviving Addiction.* Mack is a living example of what it looks like to never give up, despite experiencing some devastating stumbles along her own recovery journey. Her advice? "Brush that shit off and get back on the horse." Sage words from a brilliant actress and wise woman who devotes much of her life today to working with people in recovery from trauma and addictions.

Mine your setbacks for meaning,
but don't ever give up.

From Trauma to Transformation

Your own personal transformation in recovery is ongoing, and you should be proud of what you have survived and who you have become. Many of us are aware of the trauma that we have experienced when we start out on our recovery journey; others only uncover or identify it after we have worked with a therapist or other practitioner for some time. As we look back and begin to interpret and understand our experience, we finally understand that the numbing out with substances or behaviors was to quiet the internal voices that told us we were damaged, defective, unworthy of being cared for, and worse.

Engaging in somatic therapy is one of the best ways to understand and heal our trauma. Talk therapy is important, but our body holds on to traumatic memories too. Have you worked with a somatic therapist? Somatic therapies focus on the feedback loop that continually runs between the mind and the body. Somatic therapy connects the mind and body to facilitate healing. Some somatic practices include trauma-informed yoga, conscious dance, and other trauma-informed movement modalities. Move your body, heal your past.

We need to meet our issues where
they are trapped in our bodies.

When Truth Screams

When I was in active addiction, it was easy to stay firmly in denial when my life was going to shit. I didn't have the depth of awareness that things were bad or getting worse or the worst they had ever been. I was too busy just trying to survive. This is true regardless of whether my addiction was to substances, a love interest, or work. These days, I can live in a place of denial for a very short while if something is not going right in my world, but then the truth starts to whisper in my ear. Then it gets louder. Finally, it screams. So for a while, even though I'm hearing that we have a problem, Houston, I ignore the issue for as long as I can. I don't like it. But the longer I am in recovery, the shorter those periods of ignoring things get. When I finally admit I have to address the new thing, I always feel a sense of relief. The screaming stops. The work begins.

Recovery messes with our ability to stay in denial.
That's a good thing, by the way.

If You Are New to This Thing Called Recovery

One day you will look in the mirror and cry out to yourself, *I can't do this anymore.* And you will put down your drink, your drug, your food, your addictive relationship, your compulsive behavior. You will experiment with letting go of controlling that thing that you have been hanging on to so tightly for so long. That will be the beginning. Some other day (not necessarily the next day) you will realize that, against all odds, you have made it through another day without resorting to a maladaptive behavior that serves no helpful purpose. You will be proud that you got through the day, because it wasn't an easy day, and you will think, *Maybe there is something to this recovery thing. Maybe I can do this.* And as the days go on, even if they don't stack one on top of the other, you will, indeed, do this thing called recovery.

Recovery isn't always easy, but our lives become easier to live in recovery.

To Knit or Knot to Knit

My grandmother taught me how to knit when I was about ten. I don't have a very clear memory of the knitting lessons, but I know that I enjoyed spending one-on-one time with my "Nannie." I didn't knit anything to completion at the time; I just learned the mechanics, put the needles down, and went back to my Nancy Drew obsession.

I didn't pick up knitting needles again until I was twenty and pregnant. My claim to knitting fame to this day is a tiny, multicolored (pale pastels) baby sweater with freakishly long arms. I loved knitting it as I dreamed of the child who was coming into the world, the one who saved my life. My mom had to sew the pieces together and put the tiny buttons on it. These days, the sweater is hiding somewhere in my house. We forgot to even look for it when my daughter's own firstborn daughter arrived. My granddaughter, like her mother, was born with arms of regular length, so it wouldn't have fit her very well anyway. I still marvel that I made that sweater, and that child too.

My life in recovery is knitted together
with stitches of memories and gratitude.

• NOVEMBER 15 •

Spiritual Bypassing

I'll admit that in the past I would indulge in spiritual bypassing to dismiss or avoid complicated emotions or issues. That's when someone distances themselves or represses their feelings by explaining them away using spiritual concepts and sayings. I often chose to bypass when I was dealing with anger—an emotion that I still struggle to process sometimes. What spiritual bypassing would look like for me would be getting angry at someone—for good reason—but dismissing that anger by saying something like "I'm just going to let that person go with love." Letting someone go with love is a good practice, but there's a little bit of work to be done between the anger and letting-go parts. Spiritually bypassing prevents me from acknowledging my feelings—something that in recovery we are always trying to overcome. It's a way of hiding behind spirituality or spiritual practices. Offering up only "love and light" solutions or faking positivity to act as if our underlying feelings don't exist won't help us in the long run. I'm all for digging into the underbelly of the emotion or issue and then pulling out my spirituality card on the other side of it.

I'm becoming a lot less "love and light" and a lot more "shine the light on what's real and true" these days.

Soberful from All the Things

In her book *Soberful: Uncover a Sustainable, Fulfilling Life Free of Alcohol*, my friend Veronica Valli argues that people questioning their relationship to alcohol usually ask themselves the wrong question. She suggests that instead of asking whether our drinking is bad enough to stop, we should be asking if drinking is making our lives better. I think it's a brilliant reframe, and one that can be applied to other maladaptive behaviors as well. For example, if I were a workaholic (which I just happen to be), I can ask myself if overworking is making my life better. It's not. Regardless of any good it does for my bank account, it negatively affects my relationships, my health, and my serenity. I will always have to be diligent about getting "sober" from overworking. In which areas of your life can or should you ask the question "Is it making my life better?"

Sometimes we need to change the
question to find our answers.

Enduring Friendships

Old friends are irreplaceable. When I was a young and confused teenager, I ran away to the Yukon. I was already addicted to substances and ran with an older crowd, many of whom were dealing drugs. Mickey was a bartender just a few years older than I who, for some reason, had a soft spot for me. She knew that I was pretty messed up, and for years she was there whenever I needed her. She nursed me after a car accident, she showed up for me when I was in an abusive marriage, she even took care of my little kids when I needed help. She has also been here for me throughout all the many decades of my recovery. She is one of the people who "knew me when," and I think she is blown away that I survived my addiction and have been thriving in my recovery. I'm grateful for the care she showed me when I was at my lowest, and so glad that she loved me during my least lovable stages. I am amazed at her enduring pride in and support of my recovery. I hope that I continue to make her proud, because I'm not sure I'd be here without friends like her.

If we are lucky, the love and support of friends can guide us from turbulence through to stability.

Growing into Who We Are Meant to Be

I like to think of myself as a project, albeit an incomplete one. A lot of the pieces of me have clicked into place in recovery. I'll never be perfect and don't strive to be, but I am less often the governing problem in my own or other people's lives. Miraculously, given the self-loathing that I brought with me into recovery, I love myself always. I have mostly healthy, happy people in my life and have figured out how to love the few who aren't—from afar. I am much less reactive these days and more accepting of things. I can still lack self-confidence when I try to do something new. I've come to accept that I'm not good at conventional things like housekeeping or cooking and have released myself from those gendered expectations, fully. I can be overly sensitive about most things having to do with my family of origin, and I'm not sure that will change any time soon. It doesn't have to. I accept that some people in my life will never get my attachment to recovery, nor will they seek it for themselves. That doesn't mean that they won't someday grow into who they are meant to be too.

Because I'm still here, I'm still growing.

In Their Honor

By the time I was twenty-one, I had lost two very close friends to addiction. Tommy overdosed on heroin, and a year later Shannon drove her car off the highway while under the influence of vodka and benzodiazepines. I sometimes question why their addiction stole their lives and I survived mine, but I'll never know, of course. What I do know is that I don't take lightly the fact that I found recovery. My lifestyle in my teenage and early adult years put me at extreme risk, as it did for most of my friends at the time. None of us were in recovery; we didn't even realize that there was a solution to the substance issues that we were experiencing. When I got into recovery, I started losing friends at an even faster pace, and today, with fentanyl-tainted drugs so prevalent, people are dying at even more alarming rates. My friend Laura McKowen talks and writes about how "we are the luckiest" to have found recovery and a new way of life. I couldn't agree more, and I hope I never take for granted that I get to live my life in recovery. That I get to live, period. I recover in honor of those we have lost.

There but for the grace of god,
or the universe, go I.

• NOVEMBER 20 •

Living Life in Color

The year that I was doing chemotherapy for colon cancer was one of the best years of my life. My cancer crisis coincided with completing my PhD and moving with my husband to the West Coast. That first year in our new home, as poison medicine coursed through my veins, so too did immense gratitude and a touch of denial. My situation was dire, as indicated by my oncologist advising me to be sure to spend my time doing what I loved most, with those I loved most. Although my physical health and energy fluctuated, I was fortunate to handle the chemo quite well for the most part. Days and months were filled with daylong drives, picnicking in parks and at newfound favorite beaches, exploring quaint neighborhoods, and being completely mesmerized by the vibrant colors of our new city of gardens. As a bonus, having only ever lived together as a blended family, we got to live as just a couple for the very first time. We turned the year of cancer into a holiday and honeymoon, and at the end of it we celebrated all that and a clean bill of health too.

Sometimes we find gifts in
unexpected circumstances.

Accepting Compliments

We have so much in common, as women in recovery. I'm going to hazard a guess that you have, or in the not-too-distant past had, a hard time accepting compliments. Am I right? I'm so much better at it these days, but it's still a thing sometimes. I laughed the other day when I heard a woman in recovery say that when someone gives her a compliment, she tends to swat it away like a housefly trying to land on her. I have seen women actually *wince* when they are complimented. Many of us negate the compliment with "Oh, it's nothing" or downplay it with "I really hoped I would do better." How do we stop doing this? When one of my therapists noticed how hard it was for me to accept compliments, she gave me a three-point plan. First, I count to three after I receive a compliment. Then I say "thank you" out loud. Then I say silently to myself, *I'm grateful for the compliment.* The first few years I practiced this, it felt completely awkward. Although I no longer swat them away like flies, I still forget to receive compliments gracefully sometimes.

Thank you. That's all.

• NOVEMBER 22 •

Your Problem Is Not Your Problem

You may think that your overworking, drinking or drug use, love addiction, or your (fill in the blank) is your problem. And let's be clear, you need to do something about that thing. But it's not your *real* problem. That thing you are doing that is destroying you is what you have chosen as a solution to what really ails you. We choose maladaptive behaviors to avoid dealing with our core issues, which are usually related to unmet needs and traumas in childhood. My original core issue was childhood emotional neglect and abandonment. Drugs allowed me to live in a world where I felt that I belonged and was cared for, finally. When sexual assault and physical abuse were layered onto the original core issue, I had to use more drugs to further dissociate from my combined traumas. I thought that was the solution, until it wasn't. Recovery from substance use helped a lot, but residual trauma and still-unresolved core issues led me to become a workaholic. Work was my solution to not dealing with my shit, and it worked for a while. But then it didn't. So take it from me: as hard as it might be, if you haven't already, it's time to identify your core issues.

We don't have to identify or address our
underlying core issues on our own.
In fact, we shouldn't.

Angels in Disguise

We never know who will show up for us in our recovery, but over time we come to trust that the right people will. Many moons ago, my partner and I moved to the city where we live now, just weeks after I had undergone life-saving emergency surgery and been diagnosed with stage III colon cancer. Still weak from surgery and filled with fear for the future, I asked my husband to take me to a Twelve Step meeting. I was hurting, and although we didn't know anybody in that city, I knew we would find like-hearted people there. We needed support. I shared in that meeting that moving there was a dream come true and the culmination of years of hard work. I also shared that I was anxious about starting a yearlong journey of intense chemotherapy. I shared that we had left our kids and family behind, and that I really, really needed a friend. A woman with long hair and beautiful green eyes came up to me at the end of the meeting and said, "I am going to be your friend." I knew when she hugged me that she meant it, and we are close friends to this day.

Friends in recovery are gifts
from the universe.

We Are the Luckiest

My daughter Taryn and I are blessed to call Laura McKowen a dear friend. Laura is a beautiful writer and a right lovely human being. Her book *We Are the Luckiest: The Surprising Magic of a Sober Life* focuses quite specifically on sobriety from alcohol, but it is applicable to all sorts of sobriety and recovery. One of the things about recovery that Laura absolutely nails is embodied in her statement "One stranger who understands your experience exactly will do for you what hundreds of close friends and family who don't understand cannot." That is the wicked truth. We all come to the realization, sooner or later, that those we love don't get it. They don't get what caused us to blow up our lives (quietly or spectacularly), and they don't get the importance of what we are doing to recover from the blowup. And that's okay. Here's the thing: It's not their job to get our recovery. They have their own shit to deal with. We are better off seeking support from the professionals—and by professionals, I also mean people with lived expertise in recovery. You and me, we've got this.

It's essential that we celebrate our lives in recovery. We truly are the luckiest.

Ditching Diet Culture

I have never had an eating disorder, but I have experienced disordered eating throughout my life, mostly in the form of emotional binge eating and intermittent dieting. Christy Harrison's book *Anti-Diet* is balm for the soul for anyone struggling or confused about what is right, healthy, and appropriate when it comes to our relationships to food and to wellness. As Harrison writes, Western culture is diet culture, and it "masquerades as health, wellness and fitness." I realized just a few years ago that I had some self-loathing around my eating, and I didn't know why. On further reflection, I realized that I was being influenced by diet culture, specifically related to judging myself over whether certain foods that I loved (ice cream, hello) were bad. Although I eat healthily all the time, I was being inundated with messages about sugar that simply didn't apply to me, although I understand that some people feel they must avoid sugar. They get to do what is right for them. I personally am not comfortable with the good foods / bad foods approach, so I don't subscribe to it. I eat what I want and never judge myself. Period. It took some work to get here, but I'm so grateful for the freedom.

If you have judgment around food,
can you ask yourself if it's diet culture
that is whispering in your ear?

Easy Does It

The slogan "Easy does it" was introduced to the recovery community back in 1939 when the co-founder of AA, Bill Wilson, wrote in the Big Book of AA, "We have three little mottoes which are apropos. Here they are: *First Things First. Live and Let Live. Easy Does It.*" When I was a young woman new to recovery, the only slogan of the three that I really remember hearing repeatedly was "Easy does it." I didn't find many things in my life to be easy in the early days of recovery, but having people around me repeat the phrase on a regular basis did help. It sounded hokey to me, but it also gave me permission not to tackle absolutely everything that needed fixing in my life. There was a lot that needed fixing. I learned to practice taking things easy, and without even knowing the other two slogans, I started practicing variations of them too. In place of "First things first," I heard "Just do the next right thing," and in place of "Live and let live," I absorbed the "I can't control anyone else" principle. Combined, these three life lessons helped transform my recovery, and my life.

Easy is as easy does.

Coming Home to Ourselves

You know that feeling you get sometimes when you arrive home after a long day at work or a trip away? How you take a deep breath of relief as you walk through the door? Maybe you change quickly out of your outside clothes and slip your feet into your favorite slippers or put on your pajamas. If you are like me, you feel almost immediate comfort returning to your sacred space, knowing that you are surrounded by the people and things that make your life uniquely yours. This is what coming home to ourselves in recovery can feel like: stepping across the threshold of a new way of being, figuring out what comforts and feeds our spirit when we are no longer bound to the external stresses of maladaptive behaviors. It's important to acknowledge here that sometimes we have a lot of work to do to ensure that our literal home is a welcoming sanctuary, which can then provide the setting required for continued healing and growth. Leaving an abusive marriage was what made home safe again for me, and that, more than anything else, paved the way for me to figure out how to come home to myself personally.

Keep doing the work; all of your
unique versions of home await you.

Nondominant Handwriting Therapy

During her keynote address at our She Recovers conference in Miami, Ashley Judd introduced us to the healing practice of nondominant handwriting, something that she learned about while undergoing treatment for codependency. Since then, I and quite a few of our community members have tried it out. The technique was designed by art therapist Lucia Capacchione, and its efficacy has been proven by her longitudinal research. Evidence shows that writing with our nondominant hand helps relieve stress and anxiety. This can be a gateway to access our inner child's voice, can help us to process relationship and other issues, and can even alleviate some physical pain. It's a simple enough process. You start out thinking about an issue that is causing you stress, then you write it down as a question using your dominant hand. Then you switch the pen or pencil to your nondominant hand and write down a response to your earlier question. Are you willing to try it?

Writing with our nondominant hand can unblock suppressed emotions and invite new ideas and solutions. What have you got to lose?

• NOVEMBER 29 •

Abandoning Ourselves

I don't know who needs to know this right now, but some of those things you are doing in your life are forms of self-abandonment. Ignoring your wants and needs. Staying quiet when something unfair is happening to you or around you. Judging yourself. Staying in bad relationships—not just romantic relationships, but friendships and relationships with family members who don't have your back. Looking to others for validation. Using substances. Hanging on to other unhealthy behaviors.

There is an alternative to abandoning yourself. It's called choosing yourself. Decide you are worth coming back to. Lean into figuring out what you need, and trust that you deserve it all. You don't have to leave yourself behind anymore. Just take one tiny step back toward yourself. Do it today.

We leave ourselves behind without always knowing that is what we are doing. But we can always go back and pick ourselves up.

• NOVEMBER 30 •

One Day

One day you will look in the mirror and see a woman you don't recognize. It will be a very bad day. You will make the decision to go searching for who you were. You will look back over your past and contemplate where things went wrong and acknowledge what you did right. You will identify the patterns that ruled and (probably) still rule your life. You will go back and forth on the decision to find yourself again and put various amounts of effort into doing it, but you will be proud of even the smallest steps you take forward. You will dig a little deeper and try a little harder, and one day you will realize that you have changed a pattern that keeps you from being your highest self, and you will buy yourself flowers because damn right you are worthy.

And then one day, you will share your story with another woman who has been where you have been. Through mutual acceptance and understanding, you will both remember that you are whole and worthy and living examples of how we heal. That will be a very good day.

Take each day as it comes;
there are learnings in each one.

DECEMBER

Paying It Forward

One of the most valuable messages that I have embraced in recovery is the idea that we can only keep what we have by giving it away. No, we can't give it all away, but this concept of service is so important. The most profound thing that any of us can do to give back in our recovery is simply to show up and listen to one another. Hold space. No experience required; just bring acceptance, compassion, and understanding.

My daughter gave me a necklace that says "Selfless." I don't know about that. I know that I am entirely myself as I give what I have away. But what I do try to do is put something good into the universe—I practice random acts of kindness and try to help other people when I can. The Twelfth Step is about paying things forward. Even if you're not a Twelve Step person, you can't argue with the beauty of this. Paying it forward doesn't mean expecting anything in return. I expect nothing in return. But as you pay things forward, you should know amazing things will happen for you. They certainly have for me.

In recovery, I give away what I have . . .
because someone paid it forward to me first.

Like Mother, Like Daughter

When she was sixteen, my daughter Taryn began to mirror exactly what I had done as a teenager. Driven by unresolved trauma and low self-esteem, she became addicted to cocaine (and meth, which I had never done). She got into a relationship with a drug dealer, as I had done (with her father). When we realized what she was up to and convinced her that she needed to stop using drugs and find recovery, my partner (not her father) and I took her to our Twelve Step recovery program.

Taryn wanted recovery but wanted nothing to do with our way of doing it. She loved all of the "program" people that she had grown up around, but the Steps and meetings didn't resonate for her. Fortunately, she was committed to doing recovery and just began doing her own thing, which was a lot of therapy, yoga, and reading. She stepped away from her healing journey for a few years, but upon returning she recommitted to therapy, read a lot more, and embraced herbalism, coaching, and deeper trauma work. She designed her own patchwork for recovery. As I have. As you can.

Addiction runs in my family,
but so does recovery.

• DECEMBER 3 •

Restlessness or Anxiety?

I've been thinking recently about the difference between anxiety and restlessness. I know what anxiety is and what it feels like in my mind and in my body. I am sometimes surprised when it appears, and I don't always take care of myself as quickly as I should when it visits. I used to think that restlessness and anxiety were basically the same thing, but recently I've come to believe that whereas anxiety (for me) is a response to something going on in my environment and my life, restlessness is more of a felt sense that I need to do something, take some sort of action, reach for *more* of something. Does that make sense to you? Neither anxiety nor restlessness are inherently negative; they are just different indicators for me. Anxiety says to me, "Pay attention and practice whatever it takes to regulate this"; restlessness says, "You can go for more of whatever you want. Just do it mindfully."

I may take the rest of my life to figure out how to recognize and respond to my many conditions and feelings. And that's perfectly okay.

Labels

My personal recovery from addiction is not dependent on whether other women who are new to recovery or have been in recovery for a long time identify themselves as "alcoholics" or "addicts." I really don't care if a woman ever claims those labels, and it annoys me that some members of some recovery fellowships pressure others to identify in those ways. It's not a requirement of any Twelve Step program. Now, I do happen to refer to myself as an addict when I attend a certain recovery meeting. It's just no big deal to me, and I believe there is a certain power to saying, "My name is Dawn, and I'm an addict," because I am modeling that it's just a word, and there's no emotional charge for me when I say it. It's *not* my identity (although it was once), and I don't ever refer to myself as an addict outside of meetings. I don't need to. You don't have to identify yourself in any particular way inside or outside of any meetings or anywhere else in recovery. And if someone tries to pressure you to, send them to me.

How we identify or introduce ourselves in recovery is up to us.

Recovery Inside and Out

I was a high school dropout who went back to school after finding recovery. I stayed in school for thirteen years and earned three degrees in recovery, the last one a PhD. I don't say this to impress you, but it impresses the hell out of me. And here's the thing: I'm not unique. I know hundreds of women (and men, of course) in recovery who have as many years of recovery as me, as many degrees, as much success in their careers, who have raised children as wonderful as mine. And they all started out as broken as I was.

And here's the other thing: all the degrees, the success, the beautiful homes (ours is old, tiny, and crooked), fancy careers, beautiful children, and travel and boats and cars are just what recovery sometimes looks like on the outside for some people in recovery. I don't notice or look for those things as indicators of a strong recovery; it's what you share from your inner being that shows me that you've done the work of recovery.

I am more inspired by your
inner light than your outer life.

Anxiety

Inspirational speaker, lawyer, and author Mel Robbins says, "Anxiety is like having conspiracy theories against yourself." That resonates. I was diagnosed with generalized anxiety disorder (GAD) when my physician was treating me for burnout from overworking. I had no idea that anxiety was an actual mental health condition, and I researched it extensively. The most interesting thing I figured out was that I had probably had GAD for most of my life, and that my substance use may well have been my strategy to self-medicate and regulate my anxiety. I also learned that the coffee I had been drinking for all my time in recovery had been working against me, so I started drinking decaf and felt like a completely different person. I have stayed off caffeine, and my anxiety thanks me. If you are an anxious person, I encourage you to find out if you have an anxiety disorder, and if you do, I suggest that you reflect on the presence of anxiety in your life. It may provide answers for you as it did me. And maybe consider drinking more herbal tea.

Explore your anxiety, and then treat it with care.

• DECEMBER 7 •

Guilt

Author Sabaa Tahir tells us that there are two different kinds of guilt: "the kind that drowns you until you're useless, and the kind that fires your soul to purpose." During the years when I was physically and spiritually unwell, guilt paralyzed me. Try as I might, when I was in active addiction, I could never escape out of the cyclical pattern of remorse and self-loathing that paralyzed me into uselessness. Miraculously, after some time in recovery, that same guilt alchemized into a passion to support other women who were trying to shed guilt and build new ways of thinking about themselves. Over the years, I've become known for a saying that I came up with decades ago when I was sponsoring a lot of women in Twelve Step recovery. I still say it to a lot of women in recovery, and some days I also still say it to myself: "The shit you did was just the shit you did; it isn't who you are."

Don't drown in guilt. Swim through it until you get to the other side, and then use it to help others.

• DECEMBER 8 •

Identifying Our Core Values

I hadn't really given a lot of thought to what my core values were before coming into recovery; I'm not sure I even knew if I had any. Once in recovery, we hear a lot about the importance of identifying and acting in accordance with our values. But how do we do that? Well, let me tell you. First, find a list of personal values on the internet—there are literally thousands of such lists. Without overthinking, select ten values from the list that stick out for you. Then, spend some time pondering your short list of ten, and whittle it down to your top five. For each of those five, ask yourself what the value means for you, why it is important for you, and how it is showing up in your life currently. Give some thought to how your life is aligning with those five values, or what you need to do to better align with them. My five core values, at the moment, are family, community, diversity, making a difference, and spirituality. Values change as we do, so I revisit this exercise every few years.

Although it's a tall order, we should strive to be a living expression of our values in recovery.

When Bigger Beckons

When you've been in recovery for a while, you start asking yourself some important questions. Am I playing *small* in my life, and if so, why? Do I want to play *bigger*, and if so, why and how? The truth is, for someone who struggles with workaholism and who has experienced serious burnout, I should probably be trying to play *medium* in my life. I may have cleared the playing-small hurdle in terms of being of service to others, given that my daughter and I sparked a women's recovery movement. But I still play somewhat small in various aspects of my life. I want to write book after book after book, so playing bigger in the published author arena is on my list of things to do. I feel like I play medium in my professional life as a researcher and writer in the areas of mental health and addiction, and that feels just right; playing medium in that work supports my own mental health. I have some goals around playing bigger in personal relationships, which can always be improved and enhanced. I'll keep asking the questions about playing small or playing big. Maybe you can ask those questions of yourself as well.

May we each end up right-sized
in all areas of our lives.

The Issues Live in Our Tissues

I thought that talk therapy would heal every part of me that needed healing. I was wrong. Making sense of our past negative experiences, including our traumas, requires a sense-based healing approach. As my friend Nikki Myers, creator of Yoga 12 Step Recovery, has long said, "The issues live in our tissues." I wish this weren't true, but I do know now that stress trapped in our body is best discharged through sensorimotor (sense- and movement-based) practice. Trauma-informed yoga is one of the best modalities for healing; so, too, is breathwork (although it can be triggering if not practiced carefully). I prefer gentle movements like stretching and walking, which are easier for this asthmatic. My friend Payton will tell you that mindful dance should be in everybody's movement practice, and I tend to agree that it works well. Of course, sports and other exercise can help move energy that needs to be displaced too. As with all things in recovery, you get to choose how to move your body into wellness.

Movement is our friend when we choose movement that feels right for us.

• DECEMBER 11 •

More about Triggers

I used to think that being able to avoid my triggers would be an indicator of successful recovery. I have since learned that true healing is more about recognizing my triggers, moving through them, and ending up with a different outcome. For example, I still get triggered when I think that somebody is angry with me. In the past, I would just tell myself that I'm not responsible for other people's feelings and that I should move on. The first part of that last sentence is true. But I rarely was able to ignore other people's anger and move on. Today, when I feel, suspect, or know that someone is angry with me, I work through it. I start by pondering whether I have done something that deserved their anger, and if the answer is yes, I try to correct or make amends for it. But as importantly—or even more importantly—I have a little chat with my inner child and remind her that people can get angry with me, and it doesn't mean they will abandon me. I tell myself that over and over until it feels true. And then I can move on.

Triggers lose power when we
work through them.

• DECEMBER 12 •

Grief in Forgiveness

When I first started doing forgiveness work in my recovery, I heard a lot about how liberating forgiveness would be, whether I was forgiving myself or others. That turned out to be true, and I'm thankful. I also learned, although I never heard much about this part of it, that finding forgiveness for others can be devastatingly painful. One of the hardest things that I have worked through in my recovery is forgiving someone for not loving me. I was eighteen when we met, and I fell in love hard for the first time. I have since come to know that he cared about me, but he couldn't give me his heart, and that broke mine. It also sped up my descent into personal destruction, and I blamed him for a long time for that period of my addiction. I thought the work was forgiving him for hurting me, but it wasn't. He never wanted to hurt me. Forgiving him came many decades later, when I figured out that not having his love didn't mean I wasn't lovable; I was just meant to be loved by someone else.

Forgiveness takes time and
more than a bit of work.

Return to Self

Recovery is a practice of remembering the self, trusting the self, honoring the self, and healing and caring for the self, all of which return us to ourselves. We may not be familiar with our *self.* Patterns of neglect, trauma, and addictive behavior mean we may have never understood, trusted, or known the self. We might have avoided the self. We might have been told—and believed—someone else's version of our self. So the process of healing is one of returning to the self or recovering the self. This means that no two recoveries are the same, which means that recovery cannot be a prescriptive practice. We can look to each other for guidance or help and share modalities that have worked. We can look toward pillars, touchstones, and foundations that have worked for other people who have designed their own recovery pathways, patchworks, and practices. But the right mix of practices depends on the individual. Finding our unique recovery path is the first step in returning to our self.

I didn't know what I was looking for,
and then I found myself.

Radical Self-Like

One of the Intentions & Guiding Principles of She Recovers is "We understand that the practice of radical self-love is paramount to our well-being." An earlier version of the principles posited that radical *self-care* was paramount, but in our last revision, we decided to ramp that up a bit. The reason? Because for so many of us in recovery, the thought of self-love makes us uncomfortable. There was no way I could embrace self-love in the first year or two of my recovery; I was too used to wearing self-loathing as a cloak. If the idea of self-love is too much for you to fathom in this moment, that's okay. Trust me: stay in recovery and you'll get there. In the meantime, can you practice radical self-like? Think of three things that you like about yourself. Write them down on a sticky note and put it on your bathroom mirror. Keep thinking up things that you like about yourself; love for them and for yourself will follow.

We can like ourselves into radical self-love; it just takes practice.

Striving for Body Neutrality and Acceptance

My dear friend Ingrid Michelsen Miller is a diet recovery and weight-neutral life coach who helps women eradicate the negative thinking that so many experience around their bodies. Ingrid understands how harmful and heartbreaking it is for women to look in the mirror and ascribe negative attributes to themselves when they are not the "ideal" body type—that they have no willpower, that they're ugly. Such negative thinking, says Ingrid, is what leads many of us to embark on a new diet (or lifestyle, or clean eating plan, or cleanse, or reset, or intermittent fasting experiment). The diets or plans seldom work, and we end up with even more negative thoughts. The good news is that we can change our thought patterns, shift our focus, and retrain our brains. I've followed Ingrid's guidance on eradicating negative body thoughts, and it works. I start out with observing the negative thoughts that I have about my body and writing them down in a notebook. Then I interrogate each one and record the answers: Are the thoughts true? Do those thoughts support me? I credit this process with helping me to (mostly) achieve body acceptance and neutrality—and sometimes even embrace positive thoughts about my body. One day at a time.

Loving my body comes slowly,
but surely, in recovery.

Leaving a Legacy

It blows me away more than a little to think I might be remembered by some for founding (along with my daughter) an international women's recovery movement. I've thought about the personal belongings that I will leave behind after I'm gone and whom I will leave them to, and I hope that I leave behind a few published books about women's recovery, but I've never given much thought to leaving behind a *legacy*. I'm not even sure if I thought *normal* people like me could do that. As hokey as this sounds, the real legacy I want to leave is a legacy of love, meaning that when I die, my children, grandchildren, other family members, and dear friends will know how deeply they were loved and valued by me. Still, it's also kind of cool to think that something I helped create might also live on in other people's lives, that the accidental movement we created might support women in recovery or seeking recovery for years or decades to come. If that's what having a legacy means, then put me down for it. What kind of legacy do you want to leave?

The riches I leave behind will be counted in memories and perhaps in possibilities.

Family History

One of the hardest things I had to do in early recovery was revisit my childhood and acknowledge that it wasn't perfect. Today I operate from a place of full acceptance that my parents loved me and did the best they could, but like their parents before them, they weren't well equipped to nurture their children—my siblings and me—emotionally. We were well fed, were beautifully housed and dressed, and felt physically safe and secure growing up, always. Unfortunately, due to their own family traumas and the emotional limitations that grew out of those traumas, neither my mother nor my father were equipped to provide the emotional nurturing that we so desperately needed as little children and then as teenagers. I hate that I have to admit that, not only because of what it meant for me but what it meant for them too. My heart breaks for little me and the inner children of my siblings, but also for my parents' inner children. Intergenerational trauma (and neglect is a trauma) sucks. Thankfully, being on a recovery journey means I can bring healing forth into the next generation.

We can't rewrite history,
but we don't have to repeat it.

Not This

There is a profoundly beautiful piece of writing by author and speaker Elizabeth Gilbert that my daughter regularly shares with our recovery community—and it is changing lives. The piece of writing is titled "Not This." In it, Liz (I kind of know her a little bit through friends, so feel I can call her that) writes about how most of us confront a moment in our lives where we are forced to admit that we have ended up in the wrong place, living under circumstances that feel wrong or even bad to us. In that moment of realization, she suggests, we can have our "not this" moment. I've had more than a few of those moments: when I hit a bottom in my drug addiction, when I decided I had to leave an abusive marriage to live, when I realized that overworking was destroying my health and relationships. The important thing to know, and Elizabeth reminds us of this, is that there can be space between declaring "not this" and doing something about it. Have you experienced your own "not this" moment or moments?

"Not this" is just the beginning, but what an empowering beginning it can be.

Avoiding Shame Spirals

Shame kills women in—or seeking—substance use recovery. It almost killed me when I was in active addiction. And then, when I did find recovery, I felt engulfed by shame for things that I did or didn't do, said or didn't say in my past. I couldn't handle the guilt and shame, and I returned to using drugs for a time. My saving grace was learning that sharing those things with other women in recovery was liberating and healing, and when I started to practice that, I found my footing in recovery again. Learning how to release shame is paramount to our personal healing journeys. Learning how not to shame other women for things they do or don't do in their recovery is paramount to recovery for all of us. Evidence shows that the shame of a return to substance use often prolongs use. If you are a person in recovery from substance use, I invite you to think carefully about how you judge yourself or others for a break in recovery time. We all have to get on the same page on this. And that page reads: there's nothing to be ashamed of if you can't do recovery perfectly.

Shedding shame is the fastest way
to freedom from addiction.

I Want You to Know

My hope is that if you are struggling with anything today, you can find the strength to admit it—to yourself and to one other human being. Help is available, but you have to ask for it. You might be tired and discouraged and not believe that there is help for you in this situation, or you might doubt that you truly deserve anybody's help. I want you to know that neither of those things are true.

I want you to know that you *can* be an advocate for your own needs. My wish for you is that you realize crying out loud can sometimes be the shortcut to getting the help you need. That has been my experience. I want you to know that it was hard for me to figure out and then come to believe that I was worthy of receiving love and support from others, personally and professionally. It took me time to figure out that I wasn't defective, that I was (and still am) just a human being with struggles. My struggles were not insurmountable when I asked for help.

Our struggles start to lose their hold
over us when we ask for help.

Winter

In her beautiful book *Wintering: The Power of Rest and Retreat in Difficult Times,* Katherine May notes that winter is "a time for libraries, the muffled quiet of bookstacks and the scent of pages and dust." I absolutely concur, although since the pandemic, I've spent winters in my home library, not the public library. Winter, more than any other season, is when I dig in to reading and writing and the work of recovery (which, for me, is in large part a lot of reading and writing). When the days start getting shorter and colder, I give myself permission to get out the flannel sheets and fuzzy pajamas, the dark hot chocolate and a puzzle, and wood for our fireplace. It's in my winter cocoon that I feel drawn to look inward, less distracted by beaches and barbecues. I recover during every season, of course. But winter provides the perfect setting for the solitude that I need to really investigate where I am on my journey. Journaling, reading, and healing beside a crackling fire is magical. Try it sometime.

Winter invites us to retreat into our recovery;
I accept the invitation gladly.

Lingering Shame

Brené Brown defines *shame* as an "intensely painful feeling or experience of believing that we are flawed and therefore unworthy of love and belonging." I have read all of Brown's work, and I understand on every level—emotionally, intellectually, and spiritually—that shame is a destroyer of souls. I am also surrounded by amazing women who have platforms dedicated specifically to recognizing, understanding, and healing shame. I've explored the role of shame in my own life and worked hard to overcome it throughout my recovery. But still. When shame rears its ugly head in my life, I regress. When there is something going on in my life that I feel shame about, I go right to that place of feeling that people won't like me anymore, that I'll be judged, that they will think I'm a fake and my recovery is a lie. I know: a bit severe, right? But that's how deep shame is. I'll keep working on it and reminding myself that I'm worthy of love and belonging.

Shame pushes that "unworthy" button
even if we are in long-term recovery;
we just need to push back on it.

When Substances Don't Work

In 2000, I found myself shattered by my mother's death. Already exhausted from sixteen months of watching her battle leukemia, in the few days after her passing, I found myself completely overwhelmed with grief and confused about life. My relationship with my father was somewhat strained, and I was wracked with guilt for neglecting my children to care for my mom. My sister, who was equally devastated at our mother's passing, had her own issues and was quickly making her way to her own addiction bottom. Desperate to escape my feelings, I convinced myself that it would be a good idea—and no big deal—to treat myself to my dead mother's pain pills.

The pills helped me focus and sleep and dulled my grief. I took them, according to the directions as prescribed to my dead mother, over a period of about thirty-six hours. Then, by the grace of something greater than myself, I had a moment of clarity and threw the few remaining pills into the toilet and flushed. I recall thinking at the time that I had come too far to dishonor my dead mother, my children, or my husband by going back to using drugs. I wasn't that person anymore. That was the last time I used a substance to try to numb or bury my emotions.

There but for the grace of a higher power . . . went I.

• DECEMBER 24 •

Owning Our Stories

When we share our stories, we signal to other women that their stories matter too. I was taught that when sharing my story, I could focus on what my life was like before recovery, what happened to bring me into recovery, and what life is like now. Nowadays, when I share about my recovery, I tend to focus more on my life today because I quite love it, but I also know the power of sharing how far I have come.

Regardless of which phase of my life and recovery I am talking about, I always own and share the gritty pieces along with the pretty pieces. Although I'm sensitive about describing them so as not to trigger others, I don't shy away from acknowledging the darkest, ickiest bits of my story. I've come to learn that the things I was most hesitant to speak about eventually lost their charge as I brought them out into the light. Other women need to know that can be true for them too.

The chapters of my story are illustrated with both harm and happiness. I honor both.

• DECEMBER 25 •

Giving Back

In the recovery program where I learned how to live again, I was told that I had to give my recovery away if I wanted to keep it. I had no idea what that meant at first, but I soon came to understand the significance of paying my recovery forward, of sharing with others what has been given to me. Giving back in recovery can look different for everyone, but everything counts. Just showing up counts. Some of us are creators and program builders or become therapists, coaches, or other professionals serving people in recovery. Some of us donate to or fund recovery projects and organizations. Others of us volunteer small to significant chunks of our time to make sure that women know about or can access recovery resources in person or online. We need each one of these contributions for recovery to expand and flourish.

If my contributions are equal to the amount
of gratitude I feel for my recovery,
I'm giving back fairly.

Pajama Days

In my family, we have a tradition. It's called Pajama Day. Okay, that's not quite right. It's called Pajama Days . . . because we try to have as many of them as we can in any given week, month, or year. Pajama Days are about giving ourselves permission to be loosely clothed even if we're productive in other ways. It's about flannel, blankets, pillows, tea or popcorn, a novel, a favorite movie or TV series. It's about releasing any pressure that we might otherwise feel to look a certain way to the outside world. Pajama Days are the ultimate self-care experience.

We can still work on Pajama Days. Many of us have even proven that we can work more comfortably in our pajamas, something that we learned during the global pandemic. How many of you attended Zoom meetings in pajamas? Just because we're in pajamas doesn't mean we have to be in bed, but there's no rule against that, either. Sometimes we have back-to-back Pajama Days, which do require a shower and clean pajamas. But those are relaxing and therapeutic too.

I used to think Pajama Days were decadent.
As time goes on, I realize they are essential.

Recovery for All

We carry within us the knowledge necessary to determine our practice of recovery. As a collective, as a community, we can support each other in our individual practices of recovery.

If women from all backgrounds are to heal, if diverse women are to be empowered to build the recovery practices that are right for them, then all women need to participate in the project of healing racism within recovery communities. Racism is trauma and has everything to do with recovery. In the same manner that none of us is free until we are all free, can we really say that anyone has found recovery before we're all empowered to recover in our own way? It's impossible for real recovery to take root if we're perpetuating trauma for others. Within our recovery work, we need to do our own personal antiracism work, which for white women starts with becoming aware of and dismantling the role of white privilege and other systems of privilege in our lives.

We can heal individually, one woman at a time,
but the overarching goal is to heal the collective.

On Missing My Mom

I miss my late mom every day of my life. I miss talking to her about life and my kids and kvetching to her about all sorts of things that didn't really matter. I miss hearing her sing as she cooked or baked, and I miss eating those things that she cooked and baked. I even miss getting frustrated with her when she would tell me that I worried too much about my feelings, to which I would respond, "That kind of advice is what messed me up." I miss our laughing together, and the tears and deep conversations we shared when she was terminally ill. I feel a little guilty for all the times I told her she was to blame for my problems, because I am sure that must have hurt her. But also, I miss the way she would respond to my criticisms of her mothering skills or lack thereof by smiling at me and saying, "Well, Missy, I did the best I could. You just wait until your own girls grow up; they will have lots to say about your mothering too." True story, Mom.

I'm grateful that my mom taught me
I could be an imperfect mom.

• DECEMBER 29 •

Yoga in Recovery

My daughter Taryn has made a real impact in the recovery sphere, especially by promoting the healing power of trauma-informed care for women in recovery. Taryn is a hugely gifted yoga teacher. I've seen recovering women be completely transformed by Taryn's yoga and coaching, and I am a proud mama. I'm also not really in love with yoga. It took me quite a few years to admit that, mostly because I didn't want to disappoint my kid. I always say that I prefer "lying down" yoga. I don't like sun or moon salutations because I don't like "jumping around" yoga. But I love the breathing, the meditation that comes with yoga. In her classes, Taryn shares her passion for healing from trauma. I love the music and the readings that she shares whenever she leads a yoga session. I particularly love lying in a room full of women who are just focused on being in the moment. It's quite extraordinary. I may never be a true yogini, but I can benefit from doing yoga in my own way, at my own pace. And you can too, if you'd like.

If you can breathe and stretch,
you can do yoga. Embrace it!

Bottoms

We don't have to hit rock bottom in order to choose recovery. Some of us will. That's what it will take. From the outside, it looked like I was experiencing a lot of bottoms in my active addiction, including overdoses and suicide attempts. Although my most difficult times spanned only a decade, the intensity of my dysfunction meant that my life was often blowing up around me. I didn't know when or how to stop; I didn't even know that I could.

Those physical bottoms were not what caused me to change. Those weren't the moments when I said, "I can't do this anymore. I need to stop." One of the bottoms that finally caused me to change came many, many months after I had stopped using most of the substances that were destroying me. It came when I looked in the mirror and saw nothing but deadness in my eyes. Something about that moment woke me up, made me get serious about truly choosing recovery. Rock bottoms aren't always visible on the outside. Sometimes our spirit hits a bottom, and that's what leads us to explore recovery.

We decide what our bottom looks or feels like;
nobody else can do it for us.

• DECEMBER 31 •

Acceptance

One of my many favorite daily meditation books (aside from this one you are reading, of course) is called *Meditations for Women Who Do Too Much,* written by Anne Wilson Schaef. My two daughters gifted it to me when I was early in my recovery from workaholism, so it has special meaning for me. There are so many nuggets of wisdom throughout the book, but one sentence about acceptance has always stuck out for me, and I think of it often. Schaef wrote, "Part of learning to live our lives is developing the ability to accept what cannot be changed and learn to live creatively with those situations." I feel like that statement really sums up what my life in recovery is all about. I cannot change the things that happened or didn't happen to me as a child, can't change that I got addicted and nearly destroyed myself. I can't bring my mom back to life or take away the pain my children and other loved ones have experienced. But I can accept all those things and live creatively with them. I can do recovery and help other women recover. And guess what? You can too.

Acceptance, they say, is the solution
to all our problems. May it be so.

Reading List

Anti-Diet (Christy Harrison)

Befriending Your Body: A Self-Compassionate Approach to Freeing Yourself from Disordered Eating (Ann Saffi Biasetti)

Breaking Up with Busy: Real-Life Solutions for Overscheduled Women (Yvonne Tally)

Calling My Spirit Back (Elaine Alec)

Codependency for Dummies (Darlene Lancer)

Conquering Shame and Codependency (Darlene Lancer)

Conscious Service: Ten Ways to Reclaim Your Calling, Move beyond Burnout, and Make a Difference without Sacrificing Yourself (Elizabeth Bishop)

Creative Visualization (Shakti Gawain)

A Deeper Wisdom: The 12 Steps from a Woman's Perspective (Patricia Lynn Reilly)

Financial Recovery: Developing a Healthy Relationship with Money (Karen McCall)

Goddesses in Everywoman (Jean Shinoda Bolen)

Homecoming: Reclaiming and Healing Your Inner Child (John Bradshaw)

If You Want to Write: A Book about Art, Independence and Spirit (Brenda Ueland)

It Works, How and Why (Narcotics Anonymous)

Just for Today (Narcotics Anonymous)

Love Yourself Sober (Kate Baily and Mandy Manners)

Many Roads, One Journey: Moving Beyond the 12 Steps (Charlotte Kasl)

Meditations for Women Who Do Too Much (Anne Wilson Schaef)

Mindfulness and the Twelve Steps (Thérèse Jacobs-Stewart)

Off: Your Digital Detox for a Better Life (Tanya Goodin)

Present over Perfect: Leaving behind Frantic for a Simpler, More Soulful Way of Living (Shauna Niequist)

Quit Like a Woman: The Radical Choice to Not Drink in a Culture Obsessed with Alcohol (Holly Whitaker)

The Recovering Heart: Emotional Sobriety for Women (Beverly Conyers)

Soberful: Uncover a Sustainable, Fulfilling Life Free of Alcohol (Veronica Valli)

Untamed: The Journal (How to Quit Pleasing and Start Living) (Glennon Doyle)

We Are the Luckiest: The Surprising Magic of a Sober Life (Laura McKowen)

Wintering: The Power of Rest and Retreat in Difficult Times (Katherine May)

You Can Be an Optimist (Lucy MacDonald)

Index

D

G

H

I

P

R

S

T

U

V

W

Y

About the Author

Dr. Dawn Nickel—or "Mama Dawn," as she is affectionately known in the women's recovery space—is passionate about redefining recovery, ending the shame and stigma around it, and ensuring that women are supported to find and follow individualized pathways and patchworks of recovery. A survivor of intimate partner violence and cancer, and with over thirty-five years of recovery from substance use, Dawn currently identifies as being in active recovery from workaholism and the patriarchy. Dawn's lived experience, coupled with her academic and professional experience related to women and mental health, positions her as a highly sought-after speaker and consultant. She and her daughter Taryn Strong (also in recovery from substance use and various life challenges) "accidentally" started a worldwide women's recovery movement called She Recovers when they started a Facebook page by that name in 2011. Since then, hundreds of thousands of women have been introduced to the She Recovers philosophy and approach.

When she isn't writing, working as a health care and social policy consultant, hosting retreats, giving talks, or helping to grow the movement she started, Dawn can be found hanging out at home with her partner and family, walking or hiking with She Recovers friends, doing the odd thousand-piece puzzle, or reading. Her life goals include "graduating" therapy at some point, writing more books and a screenplay, completing her travel bucket list, and spending quality time with family, especially her precious grandchildren. Dawn understands that choosing to start her recovery journey at age twenty-seven was only the beginning; she continues to choose and practice it each and every day.

More information about the author can be found at www.dawnnickel.org.

About SHE RECOVERS® Foundation

SHE RECOVERS® Foundation is a 501(c)(3) nonprofit public charity and a global grassroots movement serving women and nonbinary individuals in or seeking recovery from life challenges including trauma, substance use, grief and loss, eating disorders, burnout and moral injury, love addiction, and mental health issues such as anxiety and depression. We are all recovering from something—and no one should have to recover alone. The organization connects women through its virtual offerings and in-person community networks, provides resources and support to help women develop their own holistic recovery patchworks, and empowers them to thrive, share their experience, and celebrate success. All efforts are designed to redefine recovery, end stigma and shame, and help more women heal.

Twenty percent of the proceeds of this book are being donated to the SHE RECOVERS Foundation.

For more information, please visit
www.sherecovers.org

About Hazelden Publishing

As part of the Hazelden Betty Ford Foundation, Hazelden Publishing offers both cutting-edge educational resources and inspirational books. Our print and digital works help guide individuals in treatment and recovery, as well as their loved ones.

Professionals who work to prevent and treat addiction also turn to Hazelden Publishing for evidence-based curricula, digital content solutions, and videos for use in schools, treatment and correctional programs, and community settings. We also offer training for implementation of our curricula.

Through published and digital works, Hazelden Publishing extends the reach of healing and hope to individuals, families, and communities affected by addiction and related issues.

Other Titles That May Interest You

A Woman's Spirit

More Meditations for Women

With quotes and meditations reflecting the strength and confidence that can come from years of living the program, *A Woman's Spirit* includes sections on challenges, faith, responsibility, expectations, changes, and purpose issues at the heart of a recovering woman's journey.

Order No. 5433

Worthy of Love

Meditations on Loving Ourselves and Others

KAREN CASEY

For those who struggle to love and be loved, *Worthy of Love* offers fifty-two wisdom-filled meditations. Favorite Hazelden author Karen Casey clarifies the varieties of love: the love we show friends, family, a lover, even ourselves.

Order No. 5005